The Purpose

The crucifixion and resurrection of Jesus is the cornerstone of our faith. ... on our behalf, we would have and be nothing. This study has humbled and convicted me. We must regularly return to the shadow of the cross, for it is here that we find power, peace, and purpose.

I pray this study will strengthen and bless you. More importantly, perhaps, I pray that these moments spent in the shadow of the cross will change you and challenge you.

May God richly bless you as you study His Word.

How to Use This Study

This Bible study was written with you in mind. It contains some special features designed to help and guide you through your study of the death, burial, and resurrection of Jesus.

Check the WORD! You will see this symbol when you are to refer to Scripture. You will need your Bible for each lesson. Choose an accurate, reliable, and readable translation. This study specifically refers to the New International Version (NIV). New King James, New American Standard, and New Revised Standard are also excellent translations. Please be careful about using The Message, Phillips, or The Living Bible. While readable, they are not accurate translations.

To the POINT! These are questions specifically designed to help you make God's Word applicable to your life today. These are "thought questions," meaning there is not one correct answer. Allow God to use these questions to strengthen your faith and more closely focus on Him.

Indicates a message from the heart. Follow carefully these inspirational thoughts which have one purpose in mind: to make God's love more real to you than ever before.

Day 1 – Day 4 Each lesson is broken into four parts. Each week as you sit down to do your lesson, begin with Day 1. The next day work on Day 2, and so forth. This way you will be able to complete each week's lesson comfortably. Spreading your work on each week's lesson over the four days will allow you to be in God's Word on a regular basis as well as help you glean God's blessings and life lessons for your heart today.

Study Group Formats

There are as many different ways to effectively use this study as there are people excited about learning God's Word. Below are three suggestions for group and/or individual study. Feel free to adapt the format to meet your group or individual study needs.

45-minute Bible Class Format

This book is an excellent tool for a Bible class study. I would recommend using the book in this setting in the following way:

1. Pray each time you begin that God's Spirit will guide you as you study and open your eyes to His Word.

2. Divide each lesson into two parts. Using the Day 1-4 markers, ask your class to study Days 1 and 2 on week one, Days 3 and 4 on week two, and so forth. There is enough material in each two-day block to meet the needs of your class time.

3. Each member of the class should be encouraged to do the lesson before the weekly class time. Your job as teacher is not to go through the material question by question but rather to organize the discussion around the central theme of that week's lesson. Choose several of the "● To the POINT!" questions that you find to be most relevant and make those the foundation of your discussion. These questions are designed to stimulate discussion and focus the class on the personal application of the lesson. Encourage the class members to share their impressions, questions, new insights, and challenges on a weekly basis.

4. Enjoy the richness of God's Word.

1 ½ – 2 hour Group Bible Study Format

This book is an excellent tool for a Group Bible Study. I would recommend using the book in this setting in the following way:

1. Pray each time you begin that God's Spirit will guide you as you study and open your eyes to His Word.

2. Do one lesson a week. There is enough material in each lesson block to meet the needs of your group study time.

3. Divide your Bible Study group into small discussion groups of 6-12 individuals. These small groups allow more active participation, enhance fellowship and a sense of belonging, and permit friendship and intimacy to grow as the groups share personal reflections of the Bible study and prayer.

WOMEN OPENING THE WORD

THE SHADOW OF THE CROSS

CASANDRA MARTIN

A 21st Century Christian Publication

ISBN-13: 978-0-89098-262-4
ISBN-10: 0-89098-262-7
Copyright © 2002 by
21st Century Christian
2809 Granny White Pike
Nashville, Tennessee 37204
All rights reserved.

Cover design byJonathan Edelhuber

Back cover illustration by Caleb Gray

4. Each small group should have a leader and an assistant leader. The responsibilities of the group leader are:

   · prepare for and lead the weekly discussion of the small group
   · encourage participation of all members of the group during the discussion

   The responsibilities of the assistant leader are:

   · contact group members weekly to encourage involvement and participation
   · be available to lead the discussion if the group leader must be absent

5. Each member of the group should be encouraged to do the lesson before the weekly class time. Your job as group leader is not to go through the material question by question but rather to organize the discussion around the central theme of that week's lesson. Choose several of the "● To the POINT!" questions that you find to be most relevant and make those the foundation of your discussion. These questions are designed to stimulate discussion and focus the class on the personal application of the lesson. Encourage the group members to share their impressions, questions, new insights, and challenges on a weekly basis.

6. Another helpful tool is to have a group leader's meeting for approximately 30 minutes prior to the beginning of class. This gives the group leaders an opportunity to share their insights, answer questions, and make sure that everyone understands the central focus of the week's study.

7. Enjoy the richness of God's Word.

Individual Study

This book is an excellent tool for a personal Bible study. I would recommend using the book in this setting in the following way:

1. Pray each time you begin that God's Spirit will guide you as you study and open your eyes to His Word.

2. Each lesson is broken into four parts. Each week as you sit down to do your lesson, begin with Day 1. The next day work on Day 2, and so forth. This way you will be able to complete each week's lesson comfortably. Spreading your work on each week's lesson over the four days will allow you to be in God's Word on a regular basis as well as help you glean God's blessings and life lessons for your heart today.

3. Enjoy the richness of God's Word.

God bless you! You are about to take an exciting journey – into the shadow of the cross!

Contents

The Cross

The crucifixion and resurrection of Jesus is the single most important event in human history. The cross stands as the delineating line between the old and the new, the past and the future, between helplessness and hope, death and life. It casts a long shadow even as we stand two thousand years removed from the actual historical event because what happened to and through Jesus during those four days is the foundation of our faith. With His death and His resurrection, Jesus secured salvation for our souls, purchased peace for our hearts, reconciled us to the Father, and healed the gaping wounds of sin. If not for His death and resurrection, we would have His great teachings but no final answer for our sin. By submitting to death on the cross, His righteousness bore the consequences of our sin. By rising on the third day, Jesus conquered death and opened the gates of heaven giving us a promise and sure hope of eternal life.

Since the crucifixion and resurrection stand at the heart of all that we as Christians believe, it is important that we take the time to once again focus on the events, and more importantly the Man, that shape the foundation of our hope. Join Jesus in the garden as blood-sweat glistens across His brow. Stand in the shadows as the betrayer approaches. Warm your hands by the fire as you listen to denials flow from those who knew and loved Him best. Feel the scourge on your back and the weight of the beam on your shoulders. Hear the cries of the women and the derision of the crowd. Listen to the gentleness in His voice as pain spreads like fire through His body. Weep as death closes Jesus' eyes. Feel your muscles strain as you push the rock in front of the tomb. Let your heart explode with joy as the resurrected Savior speaks your name.

Write Philippians 3:10-11.

____

____

____

Now go back and write your name by the word "I." Circle the ways in which you want to *know* Christ.

Lay your burden of sin down in the shadow of the cross and see with new eyes the terrible price He was willing to pay to save you. Kneel in the shadow of the cross and recognize once again His holiness and your unworthiness. Stand in the shadow of the cross and let humility, thanksgiving, and praise flow from your heart as you gaze into the eyes of the One who loved you more than His own life.

Shadow Of Submission

Thank you for choosing to make this journey. Nothing is so precious to the hearts of Christians as the story of Jesus and His great love for each of us. Nowhere is this love seen more profoundly than in the shadow of the cross. As you begin this study, ask God to prepare your mind for the lessons He wants you to learn. Ask Him for the vision to see these moments in Jesus' life with freshness and clarity. Ask Him for a heart that depends on the power revealed in the shadow of the cross.

Day 1

Back in 1872, Elizabeth Clephane penned the words to the beautiful and now much-loved hymn *Beneath the Cross of Jesus*. As its familiar melody plays through your mind, remember the words of the last verse of Elizabeth's song.

> *I take, O cross, thy shadow For my abiding place;*
> *I ask no other sunshine than The sunshine of His face;*
> *Content to let the world go by, To know no gain nor loss,*
> *My sinful self my only shame, My glory all the cross!* [1]

How many times have you sung those words? How have you allowed them to impact your heart?

____

____

Go back and slowly read the words to this beautiful hymn again – really let them sink in.

The question with which we must begin is this – are you living in the shadow of the cross? So many times we sing our songs with half an ear and listen to the Gospel in the same way. It is easy for our hearts to become dulled when the shadow of the cross is a daily reality. We move in and out of the cross' shadow in the same way that we walk through the doors in our houses. We remember the cross on Sundays, but often times, don't let it impact our lives as we go to the store or make dinner for our families.

Before we join Jesus as He approaches Golgotha, we must peel away the layers of apathy and boredom that sometimes accompany familiarity. We must look with renewed awe at our Savior and cement our faith in the salvation He provided for us on the cross.

Why do you think people lose their interest and excitement sitting in worship services week after week?

____

____

 How do you listen with freshness each time you hear the story of the cross?

____

____

> The cross should cast a long shadow over every aspect of our lives. The paradox is that living in the shadow of the cross means that we live in perfect light – the light of the Savior's love. Anything in our lives that is not defined by the shadow of the cross, not transformed by our relationship with the Lord, lies in the shadow of the world and thus in true darkness.

Of course, the cross itself is not holy or magical – it is an instrument of death the same as a gallows, an electric chair, or a needle used in lethal injection. The One who died on the cross is holy and our salvation is secured, not by magic or hocus-pocus, but by love and sacrifice. It is what He did for us on that cross that must demand our full attention.

As we begin our journey with Jesus from Gethsemane to Golgotha, let us marvel again at the blessings and privileges that are ours because of Jesus and renew our awareness of the price He paid to make us His own.

Complete the chart by looking at the Scriptures in the right-hand column and write on your heart and in the space provided what Jesus endured to give you a name and a future.

We have ...	Because Jesus ...
Peace (Romans 5:1)	Isaiah 53:5
Hope (2 Corinthians 3:12)	Matthew 27:46
Joy (1 Peter 1:8)	Mark 14:34
Acceptance (Romans 15:7)	Luke 17:25
A Home (2 Peter 3:13)	John 6:38
Love (I John 4:10)	John 15:18
Life (Colossians 2:13)	Romans 5:6-8
Forgiveness (I John 2:12)	2 Corinthians 5:21
Fullness (Colossians 2:10)	Philippians 2:7
Victory (1 Corinthians 15:57)	Revelation 5:5

The blessings of being a child of God are innumerable. The privileges are staggering. Our hearts must never become hardened to all that is ours because we wear the name of Christ. Calluses and complacency creep in when we become too comfortable with our own righteousness. As we sit in our comfortable twenty-first century homes, surrounded by luxury and technology, it is easy to see the cross as only a distant silhouette. We see the basic outline, occasionally acknowledge its significance, and go about our daily lives wearing the name of Christian like a designer label.

It is only as we near the cross, stand in its shadow, and gaze at the One who gave His life there that the hardness of our hearts melts away. That is why the journey of this study is so powerful – not because of anything that is written in this book – but because this is where the powerful love of our powerful God is most powerfully displayed.

When we stand in the shadow of the cross and truly behold all that transpired – when we hear the conversations of the people standing by His nailed feet and recognize our own voices, when we see His agony and experience His mercy, when we watch in wonder as the eternal plan of God unfolds before our eyes – our hearts will be forever transformed.

As we end our time together today, you stand at a crossroads. Choice #1: You can go through this study, hold the cross at a safe distance, and pat yourself on the back for participating in another Bible study. Choice #2: You can commit to living in the shadow of the cross and prepare your heart for the wondrous truths God has prepared for you. The journey will not always be easy – there are many difficult and painful moments we must witness – but He has promised that those who choose this path will never be the same.

Use the space below to talk with God about your decision. Ask Him to prepare your heart.

____

____

____

Go back to the words of Elizabeth's song at the beginning of this lesson and read them again. Now write Galatians 6:14.

____

____

____

Day 2

As we put on our shoes for this journey, we join Jesus in Jerusalem on the eve of His death. Jesus, the Son of God and the Son of Man, was born in Bethlehem and raised in Nazareth by Mary and Joseph. Prior to the age of thirty, we know little of our Lord's life. At thirty years old, we see Him leaving His life in Nazareth and taking on the full mantle of His ministry and purpose. For three and a half years, Jesus ministers publicly among the people of Israel. He proclaims the good news, performs countless miracles, and is the object of adoration and derision by the masses. Through it all, whether feeding the five thousand or walking on the water, Jesus has lived in the shadow of the cross knowing this is the reason He came to earth. Now the moment has come. Our burden of sin must be lifted and carried to the cross.

Read Matthew 26:30-35.

As they leave the upper room where Jesus dined with His disciples, what do Jesus and His disciples do before departing? Where does the group head?

____

What warning does He give them on the way? Why? What promise does He make?

____

____

How do Peter and the other disciples respond to Jesus' words?

____

● Why does Jesus tell Peter of his imminent denials?

____

____

All in all, it has been a difficult day for Jesus. Even as the melody of their hymn echoes through the night, the moment of His death is rapidly approaching. As night falls and the blanket of darkness enwraps Jerusalem for sleep, the darkness of the hours that lay ahead of Jesus stretch out before Him. A blanket of sorrow wraps itself around Jesus' heart and isolation makes the shadows darker, as those closest to Him still fail to understand the purpose and nature of His kingdom.

In fact, just hours earlier, about what topic had the disciples been arguing? Luke 22:24

____

Now as night is falling, the events that are about to unfold begin to weigh heavily on Jesus' mind. Having eaten what we refer to as the Last Supper with His disciples in an upper room in the southwestern part of Jerusalem, Jesus and His eleven companions walk toward the Mount of Olives on the northeastern side of the city. As they walk, Jesus once again tells them what lays ahead – the Shepherd will be stricken and the sheep will be scattered.

● In what way is Jesus your Shepherd?

____

This is where you just have to love bold, passionate, impulsive Peter. He declares that even if he must die, he will stand with Jesus and, much to their credit, the other ten disciples make the same declaration. As Jesus looks into Peter's intense eyes, He tells him that not once, but three times, denials will fall from his lips. The kingdom will not be declared by pie-in-the-sky zeal, but by faith refined in the fire of trial.

● How does Peter's experience here help you understand his words in I Peter 1:6-7?

____

____

✔ Read Luke 22:31-34.

What other information does Jesus give Peter?

____

____

● What do you learn about Satan here?

____

● What great comfort do you find here?

____

Write Romans 8:34.

____

____

Even in this darkest hour, Jesus tells Peter, and us, that God is in control. Not only is God in control, but Jesus Himself is interceding on our behalf. It is interesting that He doesn't shield Peter from the sifting anymore than we are shielded from life's pressures and stresses. Instead He prays that Peter's faith will not fail.

Why does Jesus pray for Peter's faith?

____

● In what way does your faith help you in times of sifting and distress?

____

____

Write Ephesians 6:16.

____

____

Our faith and trust in God is what will uphold us in the darkest days and shield our hearts for His glory.

Day 3

✔ Read Mark 14:1 and Exodus 12:12-14, 17, 23-27.

What time of year is it? What are the people remembering and celebrating?

____

____

____

As we join Jesus hours before His death, we must take note that it is the time of the Passover celebration in Jerusalem. The city is crowded with the faithful as they come from all over the world to remember God's deliverance of their nation from Egyptian slavery. On our calendars, Passover falls in March or April. As Jesus walks the streets of Jerusalem under the evening sky, His mind and heart turn toward the rescue He is now called upon to make – a mission to rescue us from the slavery of sin.

✔ Read Matthew 26:36-38.

Where do Jesus and the disciples go upon leaving the walls of Jerusalem?

____

What does Jesus want to do? Who does He take with Him?

____

Describe Jesus' emotional and spiritual state.

____

● In your own words, what does it mean to be *"overwhelmed with sorrow to the point of death"*?

____

____

Have you ever been overwhelmed with sorrow? What did you do in those moments?

____

____

● Why is Jesus' heart troubled and sorrowful?

____

Have you ever experienced a moment of intense dread? How does this feeling affect you physically? Emotionally? Mentally? Spiritually?

____

____

____

As Jesus and the disciples leave the Upper Room, they head for the Mount of Olives and the garden of Gethsemane. As they pass through the gate north of the temple, they enter the narrow Kidron Valley that lies between Jerusalem and the Mount of Olives. Their feet crunch on the ground as they cross over a small streambed about 6-7 feet wide. The stream which runs through the Kidron Valley is known as a winter brook which means that it remains dry most of the year except during the winter rains.[2] As they make their way across the valley, the Mount of Olives rises before them. The Mount of Olives is so named because it is covered with fruitful olive trees. Gethsemane is a garden located at the foot of the Mount of Olives. The name Gethsemane means, "oil press" because the garden is equipped with a press used by the laborers to squeeze the profitable oil from the fruit.[3] As they enter the garden, close your eyes and imagine the picture the moonlight paints for you.

How familiar was this garden to Jesus and the disciples? Luke 21:37; 22:39

____

Since the city is crowded with visitors for the Passover remembrance, it is not unusual at all to find the countryside around Jerusalem filled with travelers finding accommodations amidst the fields and the stars. Evidently, this is what Jesus and the disciples do as well, finding a quiet retreat among the olive trees in Gethsemane. They enter the garden that normally provides rest and sanctuary, yet tonight it will hold nothing but sorrow and treachery.

Knowing what is soon to happen, Jesus becomes troubled and sorrowful. This is, perhaps, His most difficult moment. The reality of the pain and agony He is about to endure, the weight of the burden of sin that He must bear, and the knowledge that He must walk this path alone, converge in Jesus' heart and mind and overwhelm Him with sorrow. We must understand that while Jesus walks into the shadow of the cross willingly and lovingly, there is nothing easy or trivial about this journey. His divine nature shudders with the understanding of the heinousness of our sin. His purity recoils from the filth of our unrighteousness. Being divine, He knows the physical agony necessary for our salvation and His young man's body shrinks back from this picture of death.

It is difficult for us to grasp how deeply this moment impacts our Savior. Jesus is intensely sad with grief and anxiety overwhelming His sorrowful soul.[4]

With the horror of what will soon take place pressing in all around Him, Jesus takes Peter, James, and John and withdraws from the rest of the group.

What does Jesus choose to do at this moment?

____

● What valuable lesson do you see in His example?

____

____

He prays. Before we ever talk about the content of this prayer, we must stop and see the beauty of our Lord on His knees. When His soul is overwhelmed, He bows His head and talks to His Father.

He bids you to do the same. When you are overwhelmed, whether by worry, grief, fear, or stress, you must learn to fall on your knees. Watch the Savior. Pour out your heart to your Father. Know that you are not alone.

● Where in your life do you feel overwhelmed?

____

____

Write Matthew 11:28.

____

____

Day 4

Night covers the land and Jesus and His friends are in the garden of Gethsemane. As darkness steals across the sky, sorrow covers the heart of our Savior. Peering between the branches of the olive trees covering the hillside, we see our Lord facing grief and pain as the horror of His imminent death floods His heart.

✔ Read Matthew 26:37-46.

What does Jesus ask Peter, James, and John to do? What do they do instead?

____

What does Jesus do? Describe His body position.

____

● What is the cup to which Jesus is referring?

____

● Since Jesus came to earth for this purpose, why does He ask for the cup to be removed?

____

____

How many times does Jesus pray this prayer?

____

What important differences do you notice between prayer one and prayer two? Matthew 26:39,42

____

____

____

● How do Jesus' words in verse 41 apply to Peter and the other disciples? How might they apply to Jesus Himself? In what way do these words apply to you?

____

____

____

____

All that He can teach them has been said. He has warned them about what is to come. He has tried to prepare them for what lies ahead. Now as the hour draws near, Jesus seeks to prepare Himself for the horrors He must face alone. Leaving His three beloved friends, He goes about a stone's throw away from them and falls down with His face to the ground and pours out His anguish to His Father. "Is there another way? Is there any other option? Does it have to be this path of pain and humiliation?" The temptation is there. He can walk away. Then we are allowed a glimpse straight into the heart of Jesus.

Write the last sentence of verse 39.

____

How do you define submission?

____

● How do we learn to bow our hearts before God with this kind of submission? What difference will it make if we do?

____

____

____

 Jesus put God's will and your need before His own sorrow and pain.

He returns to find the disciples sleeping. They evidently have little understanding of the world-altering events soon to unfold. Jesus feels the weight of loneliness even more heavily and returns to His place of prayer.

It seems from the language of His second prayer that Jesus has had an answer from His Father. "It is not possible to remove the cup. There is no other way." Jesus struggles to bring His will into complete alignment with the Father's.

From Jesus, we learn three important steps of submission.

First, we must *ask* to know God's will. It is difficult to submit to the will of God when we have not taken the time to know the will of God. We must commit ourselves to prayer and Bible study, for this is the avenue by which He reveals Himself to us. It is not wrong to bring our requests and desires to our Father. Jesus certainly did. We must, however, approach God with humility – as a servant approaches his master, or a child approaches a parent - with full understanding that though the answer may be different than what we want to hear, it is given in love.

Second, we must *accept* God's answer. How many times have you seen someone ask for advice and then turn around and do exactly what they want to do anyway? Asking and accepting are not the same thing. Accepting God's direction acknowledges Him as Lord of your heart and mind.

Third, we must *align* our wills with His. It is not God who must change. You and I must be conformed into the image of His Son. Being conformed means that pressure must be applied to change and transform our hearts so that we might more be like Him. This is not easy, but each time we submit to His will, we come closer to walking in the footsteps of Jesus.

> Submission is taking our own will or mission and making it *sub*ject or *sub*ordinate to God's will and mission.

It is important to note as we watch our Savior struggle with sorrow that this moment of submission is not an isolated one. Jesus submitted to the Father's will by leaving heaven and coming to earth in the form of a man. Throughout His ministry, He did exactly what the Father told Him to do. He resolutely set His face toward Jerusalem when the time of His death drew near. Even this moment in the garden displays the humble heart of Jesus. It would have been easy, and from human eyes of little consequence, for Jesus to avoid the garden on this night and go elsewhere for the evening. Instead, knowing that His betrayer is coming, Jesus again submits to the eternal plan, enters the garden, and places Himself in the hands of His Father.

By observing the beautiful example of our Lord, we learn that submission to the Father is a daily, continual exercise of bending and stretching our will in obedience to God. We may wonder how we can face big moments and tests of submission, but here in the garden we find the answer. We must daily practice submission in all things – kindness to the rude person who crosses our way; generosity of time, spirit, and talents as we see needs; patience with those closest to us. By daily bending in submission, our spirits learn to seek His face in all things. When moments of great testing come upon us, our daily practice will make it easier to bend our knees and our hearts to God's will even when it is most difficult.

Think of a situation in your life where you need to practice submission to God's will and Christ's example. In the space below, use the following four-step plan to move towards allowing God's will to control your actions in this situation. First, what is God's will and plan for dealing with this person or situation? Second, spend time in prayer asking God for His direction and strength as you conscientiously tell Him "Thy will be done." Third, when the moment arrives or the person crosses your path, focus on God's plan for you. React to Him and not your own emotions. Fourth, don't forget to praise Him and thank Him for being with you.

____

____

____

Luke gives us some additional information about Jesus' time in the garden.

 Read Luke 22:39-46.

What two new pieces of information are we given by Luke?

____

● In what way do you think the angel strengthens Jesus?

____

What is the significance of the blood-sweat?

____

Doctor Luke gives us another glimpse into the anguish and horror that Jesus suffers in the garden. The severe anxiety overwhelming our Lord is having physical consequences in addition to the emotional turmoil. Luke tells us that His *"sweat was like drops of blood falling to the ground."* (Luke 22:44) The phrase "drops of blood" is translated from the Greek word *thromboi*, which means "clots of blood."[5] Luke seems to be referring to a medical condition called hematidrosis that can occur in situations of extreme stress. The unbearable stress causes the small blood vessels under the skin to bleed into the sweat glands. What then exudes from of the body is blood-tinged perspiration. While the amount of blood that Jesus loses at this time is minimal, hematidrosis does cause the skin to become sensitive and tender.[6]

Look at Genesis 3:19. What is one of the punishments laid on man for his sin?

____

As the sin of mankind is laid on Jesus, He too sweats, but not just any sweat. His sweat is mingled with the blood that will cover our sin.

---

1 Clephane, p314
2 Clarke, p946
3 Davis, p268
4 Strong, p324
5 Coffman, *Luke*, p431
6 Strobel, p195

Shadow Of Betrayal

As Jesus prays in the garden struggling with what is to come, a friend and associate of the Master prepares to turn Him over to Jewish authorities. This week we will hold our breath in horror as the betrayer seeks to mask his deception with a kiss. As those who promised to stand and die with Him only a few hours earlier flee in fear, Jesus is arrested and bound by those who seek to silence Him through death.

Day 1

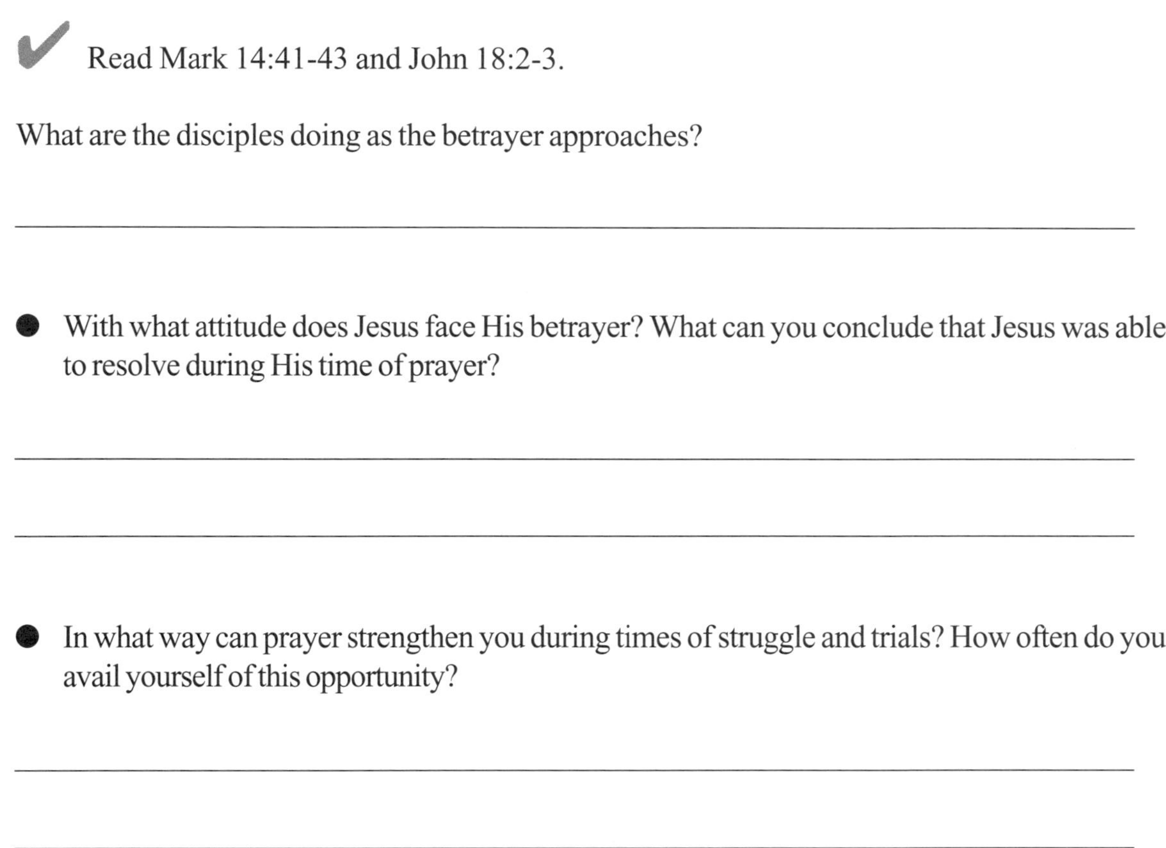

Read Mark 14:41-43 and John 18:2-3.

What are the disciples doing as the betrayer approaches?

____

● With what attitude does Jesus face His betrayer? What can you conclude that Jesus was able to resolve during His time of prayer?

____

____

● In what way can prayer strengthen you during times of struggle and trials? How often do you avail yourself of this opportunity?

____

____

Prayer is our lifeline to the Father. By going to God in prayer during the storms of life, He can calm our fears with His peace, secure our hearts with His promises, and strengthen our souls with His power.

Who is the betrayer? How does he know where to find Jesus?

____

Who does he bring with him? What are they carrying?

____

____

It is very late at night. Darkness cloaks the garden but it does not bring stillness or rest. Jesus finishes His time in prayer and, having fully submitted His will to the Father, He wakes the sleeping disciples. As they open their heavy eyes, Jesus announces that the hour has come – the hour of His betrayal, the hour of His death, the hour of our salvation.

Amazingly, Jesus does not run and hide from those coming to seek His life. Instead, with calm confidence, He rouses Peter, James, and John and steps forward to meet his betrayer.

Imagine the scene for just a moment. It is dark, the middle of the night. There are no streetlights or passing cars. Outside the city the blackness of night is a blanket pierced only by the stars and the moon. As Jesus wakes the disciples, a large crowd enters the garden. Carrying torches and lanterns, they prepare to search the shadows of the olive grove for Jesus and His followers. As the disciples stare in shock at the armed mob coming their direction, another wave of surprise washes over them. At the head of the group, leading the detachment of soldiers is Judas, one of their own.

Who is Judas? What would lead him to make such a vile move? What can we learn from this man? Let us look into the Gospels and learn about the man whose name is now synonymous with deceit and treachery.

Look at each of the following Scriptures and record what you discover about Judas.

Mark 3:13-19 ____

John 6:70-71 ____

John 12:4-6 ____

How do you picture Judas? Painters through time have portrayed him as a swarthy man, dark eyes filled with greed, a furtive look of betrayal playing on his face. This may be your picture as well but actually, we are given very little information about the man who played such a dastardly role in the death of our Lord.

Judas is the son of Simon Iscariot. The surname Iscariot identifies his family as being from Kerioth, a city in the tribal land of Judah. Thus, while Peter and the rest are from Galilee, Judas is from Judah near Jerusalem.[1]

Our first glimpse of Judas is at the calling of the Twelve to be apostles. He is among those selected to work and move with Jesus during His ministry. Mark 3:13 states that Jesus *"called to him those he wanted…"* Jesus wanted Judas to learn and walk at His side. He, along with the other eleven apostles, is given power and authority to heal the sick and drive out demons. He watches as Jesus feeds the five thousand and makes the blind to see and the lame to walk. He hears the parables and watches as Lazarus comes out of the tomb. Yet, watching the reality of Jesus' power seems to do little to touch the heart of Judas.

Jesus' own words early in His ministry seem to indicate the kind of heart that Judas possesses. After witnessing the miracle of the loaves and fish, Judas is in the boat with the other disciples as the wind blows across the Sea of Galilee. He, too, watches in terror and amazement as Jesus approaches them walking on the water. The next day, as disappointment and frustration swell through the crowd at Jesus' difficult teachings about discipleship, He turns to the Twelve, including Judas, and asks if they too wish to leave. Here Peter makes his profound confession of faith that Jesus is the Holy One of God. In contrast to the acknowledgement that He is indeed divine, Jesus gives us a glimpse into the heart of one of those He has specially chosen. One of them is a devil.

● Is it possible to have knowledge about Jesus and that knowledge not touch your heart? Explain. How do you guard against this?

____

____

It is not enough to know about Jesus. We must allow that knowledge to shape our actions, thoughts, words, and hearts into the image of the One who saves us.

In John 12, we are told that Judas holds a place of trust and confidence among the Twelve. He is the keeper of the moneybag – the group's treasurer. There are individuals donating money to support Jesus in His ministry, and Judas is responsible for the handling of these funds. Here, though, we are given another insight into the character of Judas. Judas is a thief. He secretly skims money off the donations given for Jesus' support. It seems unlikely that the others, save Jesus, know of Judas' dishonesty until after his betrayal.

The Holy Spirit also describes another more subtle heart trait here. Judas knows how to couch his greed in religious terminology. His avarice and callous indifference to the needs of the poor are carefully hidden in appropriate religious rhetoric. This tells us that Judas is an intelligent man who knows, very honestly, how to play the game. Today, we probably would call him a successful businessman.

What opportunities does Judas squander?

____

____

● What opportunities has Jesus given you? How do you ensure that you take full advantage of these opportunities?

____

____

● What do we forfeit if we do squander His blessings and opportunities?

____

____

Day 2

Before we go back to the mob trampling through the garden, we must understand who is coming for Jesus and the plot that brings them to this moment.

Write Mark 8:31.

____

____

____

✔ Read John 11:45-53.

Why is a meeting of the Sanhedrin called?

____

● Why does the Jewish leadership reject Jesus instead of accepting Him as the Messiah? In what way are these many of the same reasons that people reject Jesus today?

____

____

Who is the high priest? What prophecy does he make concerning Jesus' death?

____

● What is Caiaphas' perception of the words he speaks? What message does God want us to understand through Caiaphas' words?

____

____

What plan begins to take shape at this meeting?

____

The Sanhedrin is the ruling body of the Jewish people. It consists of seventy elders under the rule of one high priest and has authority over religious and civil matters in Israel. They oversee worship at the temple and much of daily life among the Jewish people. At this time, the Sanhedrin is under the authority of the Roman Empire and the Roman governor in Judea, Pontius Pilate, limits their power.

The body of the Sanhedrin primarily consists of members of two religious sects – the Pharisees and the Sadducees. The Pharisees believe in strict interpretation of the Law of Moses. To help them do this, they have created a complex set of oral traditions that seek to guide every situation possible in Jewish life. Gradually, the Pharisees' traditions have taken on more importance than the Law itself, as they seek to bind these oral laws on the hearts of the people. Jesus condemns the Pharisees more than any other group during His ministry.

The Sadducees, of which the high priest at this time is a member, have an all-together different point of view. Among the most educated and wealthy in Jewish society, the Sadducees do not believe in the resurrection or angels and seem more interested in political and material power than true godliness. Jesus harshly criticizes their attitude as well.

✔ Read Luke 7:29-30.

● How does the attitude of the Pharisees and the experts in the law differ from that of the common people?

____

____

● What is God's purpose for you? In what way are you accepting or rejecting that purpose?

____

____

____

Normally ideological enemies, the Pharisees and the Sadducees come together to oppose one they perceive as a common foe – Jesus. The Sanhedrin does not seem particularly worried about whether or not Jesus is the Christ. Rather, they are worried about their personal position and power as Jesus' teachings and miracles cement a growing number of faithful among the people.

Caiaphas points out to the Sanhedrin the specific solution to their problem. Kill Jesus and His followers will fall away. Rid yourself of this one man, he astutely suggests, and the nation, as well as your positions, will be saved. With these words, Jesus' death warrant is signed.

✔ Read Mark 14:1-2, 10-11 and Matthew 26:14-16.

When and how are the members of the Sanhedrin seeking to kill Jesus?

____

What surprising offer causes them to change their plans? How much money do they agree to pay?

____

● Why do you think that Judas decides to betray Jesus?

____

____

The plot is fixed, and the Jewish leadership is looking for an opportunity to kill Jesus in secret. They plan to wait until after the Passover celebration so that there will be no riot among the people. Imagine their surprise when one of Jesus' closest followers approaches them with an amazing offer – he will hand Jesus over to them for a price. Delighted at their good fortune, they agree to pay Judas thirty pieces of silver.

While on the surface thirty pieces of silver may seem like a handsome price, it is actually quite a paltry sum. Moreover, the prophets had foretold the exact amount of the betrayal price.

Read Exodus 21:32. What is the monetary value of a slave's life under the Mosaic Law?

____

Read Zechariah 11:12-13. What insignificant value does the flock place on the services of the Shepherd?

____

Thirty pieces of silver is the customary price for a slave under the Law of Moses. The Shepherd described by Zechariah is insulted by the amount. Translated into modern monetary terms, Judas is paid about ten dollars for betraying the Son of God.[2]

● Where in our society do you see the Judas principle played out – exchanging the true riches of God's kingdom for the wealth of this world? In what ways can we be guilty of this as well?

____

____

Write Matthew 16:26.

____

____

Day 3

As the approaching crowd breaks the quiet of the garden, their torchlight reveals the faces of those coming to arrest Jesus. I imagine that the apostles widened their eyes in disbelief as they spot Judas leading the soldiers toward Jesus. Even though Jesus had warned them of a traitor in their midst, as recently as this night's meal, they do not recognize the betrayer among them.

✔ Read John 13:18-30.

Why does Jesus tell the apostles that one among them will betray Him?

____

How does Jesus feel about being betrayed by one of His own?

____

How do the disciples react to Jesus' announcement?

____

Who is the disciple whom Jesus loved? What does Peter ask him to ask Jesus?

____

● What happens as Judas takes the bread? What does this mean?

____

What does Jesus tell Judas to do? How do the other apostles understand Jesus' instructions?

____

To prepare them for the shockwaves to come, Jesus tells His disciples that one of them will betray Him into the hands of sinners. Even as He is troubled by the reality of disloyalty among those closest to Him, He seeks to steady the faith of the remaining eleven. As the next few hours and days unfold, His teaching of what will soon take place will help the apostles understand that Jesus is the Son of God and that the Father's will is in control, not the hatred of men. As each disciple looks at the Lord and asks, *"Surely not I, Lord?"* (Matthew 26:22), Peter leans over to John, who is sitting close to Jesus, and tells him to ask Jesus who He means. Seated on the floor around the table, John leans back against Jesus and questions Him about the identity of the betrayer. Giving the dipped piece of bread to Judas accomplishes two purposes. First, He clearly identifies, at least to John, Judas as the betrayer. Second, this is evidently Judas' last moment to reconsider his fateful choice. Instead of falling before Jesus in repentance and sorrow, he takes the bread from his Lord's hand and his alliance with Satan is sealed.

Even as Judas arises to meet his conspirators, the rest of the apostles do not suspect him. Upon hearing Jesus tell Judas, *"What you are about to do, do quickly,"* (John 13:27) the eleven assume that Judas is being sent to finish some undone task necessary for the observance of the Passover. Despite the fact that throughout the Gospels Judas is clearly labeled as the betrayer, here, just hours before His arrest, the rest of the apostles seem unaware of Judas' treachery.

✔ Read Psalm 55:12-14.

In what way do David's words foreshadow Jesus and Judas?

____

____

● Have you ever felt betrayed by a friend? What emotions does betrayal bring to the surface?

____

____

● What lessons do you learn from Jesus' treatment of Judas?

____

____

✔ Read Matthew 26:47-49.

What signal does Judas use to identify Jesus? Why do they think that a signal is going to be necessary?

____

____

How does Judas greet Jesus? What does this title mean?

____

Thinking that Jesus and His followers would scatter and hide at the appearance of the chief priests and Roman soldiers, Judas prearranges a signal with the leaders of the group. A kiss will mark Jesus as the one they seek. As they arrive, however, Jesus does not run, but rather steps forward to meet his captors. Judas approaches Jesus and addresses Him as *"Rabbi."* Rabbi is the Hebrew word for teacher. Then Judas comes close, as is customary between a student and a teacher, and kisses Him. A sweet symbol of friendship used as a signal for deceit.

Write Jesus words in Matthew 26:50. Circle how He addresses Judas.

____

● How can Jesus still address Judas as friend in the face of his betrayal? What truth does our Lord want you to understand?

____

____

● In what way is Jesus your Teacher and Friend? In what ways has He called you to be a teacher and friend?

____

____

Day 4

✔ Read John 18:4-11.

What surprising question does Jesus ask the mob?

____

How does the large group respond when Jesus identifies Himself? Why?

____

____

____

How does Jesus seek to protect the apostles? What does this suggest to you about the intentions of the Sanhedrin?

____

____

What does Peter do? Why?

____

How does Jesus respond to Peter's actions? See also Luke 22:51

____

____

Jesus approaches the gathering contingent of temple guards, Roman soldiers, and Jewish officials with peaceful confidence. Instead of quaking with fear as they had expected, Jesus calmly asks them whom they are seeking and identifies Himself as Jesus of Nazareth. This completely stuns the mob. Having anticipated a fight, they are now faced with a man who not only stands fearlessly before them, but also addresses them with a strange calm. Whether in awe or in fear, the entire cohort of men fall on their faces to the ground before the Son of God.

● Read Philippians 4:4-7. In what way does the peace of God transcend the world's understanding?

____

____

● How can this kind of peace help you face life's trials?

____

____

Peter rises to defend our Lord. Taking the short sword he has brought with him, he swings and takes aim at the ones he deems responsible for this ambush – the chief priests. He manages to strike the servant of the high priest and chops off his right ear. Jesus immediately rebukes Peter. Peter has again misunderstood Jesus' mission. Here we see the fruit of Jesus' time in prayer. He tells Peter that He must drink the cup the Father has placed before Him. No hesitancy. No wavering. Jesus will walk in obedience for the Father's glory. Luke tells us that Jesus heals the man's ear – a miracle that seems to have no discernable impact on the men bent on taking Jesus into custody.

● Read Matthew 26:52-54. What power does Jesus have at His disposal? Why does He choose not to exercise this power?

____

____

✔ Read Luke 22:52-53.

What does Jesus then ask the men who have come to arrest Him?

____

What paradox in their behavior does He reveal?

____

● How does John 3:19-20 explain Jesus' statement that their hour is defined by darkness?

____

____

Jesus shows the chief priests and elders that He understands their true motives. He shows them with this one statement that their claims to the Roman officials that He is leading a rebellion are false. If they are true, then they have participated in the insurrection because He has been teaching in the temple under their watchful eyes. He then explains that the darkness of the night reveals the blackness of their hearts. Their true motivation is evil, pure and simple.

● In what way does Jesus stand in contrast to the darkness? John 8:12; I John 1:5

____

● In what way does Jesus call you to stand in contrast to the darkness? Matthew 5:14-16
How are you ensuring that your light is shining brightly for Him?

____

____

> Light brings peace, warmth, comfort, direction, and healing. The light of Jesus' love provides all these things for your heart. He calls you to reflect His light and shine hope into the darkness and desperation that clouds the hearts of those around you.

✔ Read John 18:12 and then write Mark 14:50.

____

In the midst of all this activity, the Roman soldiers step forward to arrest Jesus. The prescribed Roman procedure for making an arrest would involve taking Jesus' right arm and twisting it up behind His back until His hand touches His shoulder blades. At the same time, a soldier would stomp his heel into the right instep to prevent attempted escape.[3] Thus, Jesus is bound much like modern-day criminals are handcuffed.

When it is obvious that Jesus is not going to offer any resistance to His arrest and that perhaps their own lives and liberty are at stake, the disciples desert Jesus and flee into the darkness.

As the company of men prepares to take Jesus to waiting Jewish officials, we are given one more piece of eyewitness information.

✔ Read Mark 14:51-52.

While we are not specifically told, most sources identify this young man as the writer of this Gospel – John Mark. Perhaps in the garden to warn Jesus of the coming arrest, the officials attempt to seize even this young follower of our Lord. He manages to escape by leaving his cloak behind and flees naked into the night.

What additional burden does the disciples' desertion lay on Jesus' heart?

____

● How does loneliness make our trials seem more difficult to bear? How can you ease some else's burden of loneliness this week?

____

____

---

1 Lockyer, *All the Apostles of the Bible,* p101
2 Lockyer, *All the Apostles of the Bible,* p109
3 Bishop, p375

Shadow Of Denial

Jesus enters the garden of Gethsemane surrounded by disciples committed to standing by Him even to death. He leaves the garden bound by Roman soldiers without even one follower by His side. The ultimate purpose of His earthly mission is now beginning to unfold. Jesus is led away to stand trial before His accusers. Actually, Jesus endures six trials in the course of about twelve hours – three Jewish and three Roman. This week we will sit among the Sanhedrin as the Jewish leadership condemns to death the promised Messiah.

Day 1

✔ Read John 18:12-14.

To whom is Jesus first taken? Who is his son-in-law?

____

What does John remind us that Caiaphas has already decided?

____

What clue is John giving you about the fairness of Jesus' trials?

____

Jesus is led from the garden of Gethsemane to the wealthy home of Annas. Annas is a Sadducee who at one time was high priest in the temple in Jerusalem. By this time in Israelite history, the role of high priest is not just religious in nature. It has taken on a decidedly political flavor. During this time of Roman occupation in Judea, the office of high priest is filled by appointment from the emperor. In the case of Annas, Emperor Quirinus appointed him high priest in 7 A.D.[1] About nine years later, Tiberius removed Annas from office for putting to death a young man deemed guilty of not honoring the Sabbath.[2] While Rome had given the Sanhedrin and the high priest much latitude in handling Jewish matters, they were stripped of the power to carry out the death penalty. At the time of Jesus' arrest and trials, this restriction is still in place.

Despite being removed from office, Annas retains great power. The Jews believe that a man is high priest for life and therefore, despite not having Rome's official recognition, he is honored as the true high priest among the Jewish people. The role of high priest is rotated among several of Annas' sons and sons-in-law while much of the true power remains in Annas' hands.

As a reminder that the deck is already stacked against Jesus, John tells us that Caiaphas has already pronounced judgment in Jesus' case. He must die. The trials that go on through the night are not meant to be fair and result in justice. They are vehicles to bring about Jesus' death.

✔ Read John 18:15-18.

Which two disciples follow Jesus to the high priest's residence?

____

How do they each gain admittance into the courtyard?

____

What is the weather like? What does Peter do as a result?

____

Who questions Peter? What is his response?

____

Initially deserted by all of the disciples, we see two of the apostles arrive at the home of Annas as Jesus is being led in to stand before this powerful man. The man John refers to as "another disciple" is almost certainly the apostle himself as he frequently refers to himself in the third person rather than by name throughout his Gospel. Known by the high priest, John is allowed admittance into the courtyard area of Annas' residence.

● Are there ever times when it is difficult for you to stand beside Jesus? What can you learn from John's example that will help you face those moments?

____

____

Peter also follows Jesus from afar. When he reaches Annas' residence, he is not allowed in and is forced to wait outside the gate. Somehow John becomes aware of Peter's presence and vouches for his friend. Upon John's intervention, Peter is allowed into the courtyard area. As he enters, the servant girl assigned to admitting visitors into Annas' home asks a question that fills him with panic – *"You are not one of his disciples, are you?"* With heavy hearts, we hear Peter say, *"I am not."*

● How can fear make your faith crumble?

____

____

When your legs feel like they're going to buckle with fear, it is a hint to fall on your knees in prayer.

Day 2

As Peter stands by the fire in the courtyard trying to chase the chill from his hands and his heart, Annas is turning up the heat on Jesus.

✔ Read John 18:19-24.

About what does Annas question Jesus?

____

How does Jesus respond to his probing?

____

____

What does one of Annas' officials do? Why?

____

How does Jesus answer him?

____

In a somewhat informal hearing, Annas questions Jesus about His teachings and His disciples. What Annas is seeking is unclear. Perhaps more than information about Jesus' teaching, Annas is seeking to intimidate Jesus. Annas' character suggests that he is somewhat of a bully. Jesus calmly responds that He has spoken openly before all the Jews. He is not guilty of secretly planning a rebellion. In fact, as there have consistently been Pharisees, Sadducees, and experts and teachers of the law following Jesus to try and trap Him in His answers, Annas should just ask his own men to explain the content of His message.

The response to Jesus' words is a slap across His face. Each step through this night will bring physical pain to our Lord.

● Are there religious bullies today? What is the best way to equip ourselves to handle these situations?

____

____

Annas, unable to get from Jesus what he desires, sends Him to Caiaphas.

✔ Read Matthew 26:57-63a and Mark 14:53-61a.

What kind of evidence is the Sanhedrin seeking?

____

Look at Deuteronomy 19:15. What minimum standard are the leaders trying to meet? What difficulties do they encounter?

____

What charge finally surfaces late into the proceedings? Is it a valid charge?

● Read John 2:18-22. To what temple is Jesus referring? What significance is there in this claim being brought to light at this time?

How does Jesus respond to all the false allegations swirling around Him?

As word goes out to the Sanhedrin, members of the council arrive at Caiaphas' home. They are seeking a basis by which they can approach the Roman governor and demand Jesus be put to death. Evidently, Caiaphas and Annas live close to each other because Peter stays by the fire in the courtyard while the second trial commences.

It is important to recognize the illegal nature of the Jewish trials that Jesus faces. Holding the trial at night, striking the prisoner before judgment has been reached, and knowingly accepting false testimony make the whole process Jesus is enduring highly suspect. But remember, the Jewish leadership is not convening this trial to discover the truth and exact justice. They come together at this dark hour because they seek to cloak their plot to kill Jesus with a semblance of legitimacy.

As the night progresses, the plan to convict Jesus unravels. They cannot even get two false witnesses to agree on a lie. The only accusation that surfaces at all is a twisted version of Jesus' words about rebuilding the temple. Even here the false witnesses cannot agree. The only way that Caiaphas can salvage this deteriorating process is if Jesus will speak and thus condemn Himself. Caiaphas challenges Jesus to answer the false charges that have been thrown at Him. Jesus remains silent.

● Obviously, we are not as blameless as Jesus. What can you do, however, to maintain a good reputation?

Fill in the blanks in the following passage from Philippians 2:14-16a. (NIV)

"Do _________________________ without _________________________ or

_________________________, so that you may become _________________________

and _________________________, children of _________________________ without fault in a

_________________________ and _________________________ generation in which you

_________________________ like _________________________ in the universe as you hold

out the _________________________ of _________________________..."

Day 3

With the case against Jesus falling apart, Caiaphas is in trouble. If he is unable to convict Jesus on charges that will stand before the Roman governor, Jesus will be set free, strengthened by the Jewish leadership's inability to find any fault in Him. Jesus' silence only further inflames him. Instead of the usual begging and pleading done by prisoners, Jesus remains calm and peaceful. Finally, Caiaphas looks into the face of Jesus and demands an answer.

Read Matthew 26:63b-66 and Mark 14:61b-64.

What question does Caiaphas ask Jesus?

____

· Why is it significant that the trial of Jesus hangs on this question?

____

____

● What is Jesus' answer? Specifically, what two words does He use to answer this query in Mark 14:62? What is the importance of these words?

What future picture of Himself does Jesus describe to Caiaphas?

How does the high priest react to Jesus' statement?

On what charge does the Jewish leadership finally convict Jesus? What punishment do they impose?

All of their plotting comes down to one question – "Are you the Christ, the Son of God?" Here, in a nutshell, is the crux of Jesus' ministry. God will not allow Jesus to be put to death for any reason except the truth. Israel's rejection of her Messiah will be clear and awful. This, of course, is not the first time the Jews have asked this of Jesus.

✔ Read John 10:24-26.

What answer does Jesus give at this time? What proof does He offer?

It is easy to miss the significance of Jesus' answer to Caiaphas' questioning about His identity. I imagine that Jesus looks His accusers straight in the eye and answers, *"I am."* To the Jewish mind, these two words are loaded with divine meaning.

✔ Read Exodus 3:14 and John 8:54-59.

What name does God reveal to Moses as His personal and covenant name?

____

How had the Jews previously reacted when Jesus claimed this name?

____

In responding this way to Caiaphas' question, Jesus is proclaiming that He is one with God.

Now we come to the most precious, solemn moment in life. How you answer this question determines not only your course through this life, but the eternal destiny of your soul.

Do you believe that Jesus is the Christ, the Son of God?

____

In professing that Jesus is the Son of God, you must turn your heart to obedience – obedience to His plan for your salvation, obedience in your walk as His child, obedience in sharing His truth with others.

As Jesus describes a scene in which He will one day be seated in judgment next to the Father, Caiaphas tears his clothes to demonstrate the seriousness of Jesus' words. It is interesting to note that Caiaphas and the Sanhedrin do not even seem to pause and consider whether Jesus is telling the truth. Instead they use His own words to convict Him of blasphemy.

Define blasphemy.

____

● Is Jesus guilty of blasphemy? Explain.

____

Although the men of the Sanhedrin have waded through lies and false testimony, met in the dark of night, sought a conviction instead of the truth, and torn the robes of the high priest which were never to be torn (Leviticus 21:10), they now stand up in defense of the name of God. Such irony! They, who by their very actions deny the righteousness of God, now stand in judgment of His pure and blameless Son. They sentence Jesus to death.

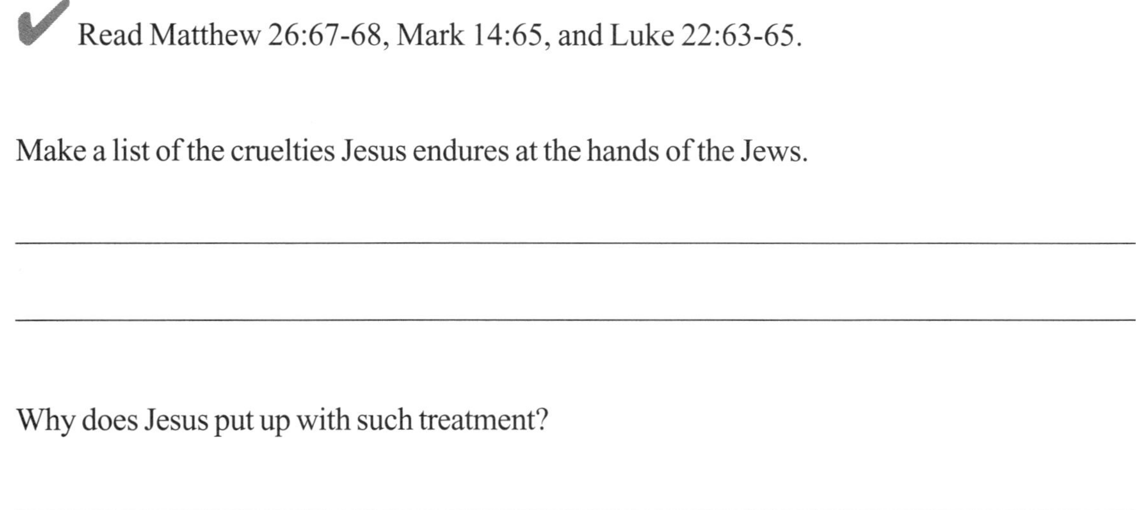 Read Matthew 26:67-68, Mark 14:65, and Luke 22:63-65.

Make a list of the cruelties Jesus endures at the hands of the Jews.

____

____

Why does Jesus put up with such treatment?

____

Stop and imagine the scene for a moment. It is nearing dawn. Jesus has been betrayed by one of His closest companions. In anguish, He pours out His heart to His Father, sorrow and distress flooding over Him mentally and physically in the form of the blood-sweat. He stands all night before those who were supposed to welcome Him and prepare the people for His kingdom. Instead, they break every trust to illegally try and convict Him. Now exhausted and emotionally spent, He endures being slapped, blindfolded, punched, spit upon, and insulted because He wants to walk the path to the cross for you. Think how much love and restraint Jesus shows at this moment. Imagine the Son of God being made into a punching bag by men He is willing to die to save. And this is only the beginning.

Stop now and thank Jesus for His incredible love for you.

Day 4

As Jesus' integrity is being weighed before members of the Sanhedrin, Peter's integrity is being weighed in the courtyard below.

Read Matthew 26:71-72, Mark 14:68b-70a, and John 18:25.

What do you notice about Peter's movements around the courtyard?

____

In what way is Peter's denial more emphatic this second time? Why?

____

Peter seems to be one of those men who, the more they try to be inconspicuous, the more they stand out. After being questioned at the gate by the servant girl and denying being a disciple of Jesus, Peter settles into the courtyard to see what will become of his Lord. It seems that he tries to stay out of the way by heading to another entryway away from the girl that has already questioned him about his relationship with Jesus. As he warms himself by a communal fire, something about Peter causes those around him to once again question where his loyalties lie. This time, with an oath, Peter denies even knowing Jesus.

● Besides oral denials, are there other ways that we can deny knowing Jesus? Explain.

____

____

____

Write Matthew 10:32-33.

____

____

____

✔ Read Matthew 26:73-75, Mark 14:70b-72, Luke 22:59-60, and John 18:26-27.

How much time elapses after Peter's second denial?

____

What two things about Peter raise suspicion in those around him?

Who recognizes Peter from the garden? What kind of fear might this have raised in Peter?

How violent is Peter's third denial?

What happens immediately after Peter speaks? Of what is Peter reminded?

About an hour elapses as the Sanhedrin attempts to formulate a charge against Jesus. Peter, sitting with others in the courtyard who are waiting to see what will happen, is confronted yet again about his relationship to Jesus. This time the accusations are somewhat different. Rather than general questions about Peter's contact with Jesus, the suspicions raised here spring from specific information about Peter. In chatting with the people by the fire, his heavy accent has revealed that he is not from Jerusalem, but from Galilee. Since the Lord is known as Jesus of Nazareth among the Jews, Peter's hometown causes some to suspect that he has followed Jesus here from the north. While this discussion is going on, another man, a relative of Malchus whose ear Peter had sliced off, recognizes Peter from the garden and challenges him concerning his presence there. Panic spreads through Peter's heart. This time Peter vehemently denies knowing Jesus, even swearing and cursing to underscore his point. Immediately the cock crows and as the sound fills the early morning air, realization floods Peter's stunned mind. Just as Jesus had said, Peter has denied Him three times.

✔ Read Luke 22:59-62.

What does Jesus do as the rooster crows?

What does Peter do then? What does this tell you about Peter's heart?

● Have you ever felt ashamed and wept bitterly before the Lord? Explain.

____

____

● What promise and consolation do we have in those moments? I John 1:9

____

____

As the rooster's cry announces the dawn, a cry strangles Peter's voice. As the truth dawns in Peter's mind about what has just transpired, he catches a glimpse of Jesus. Jesus is looking straight at him with sorrow and wisdom. Peter, who had so many times before pledged his unswerving loyalty, has failed his Lord. He leaves the courtyard of the high priest's home weeping bitterly.

● When Jesus looks straight at you, what do you want Him to see? What are you doing to ensure that is what He sees?

____

____

Jesus, having already been through two Jewish trials before both Annas and Caiaphas, is now on His way to facing His third trial.

✔ Read Luke 22:66-71 and Matthew 27:1.

When does the final trial convene? Who is present?

____

____

What two questions do they again ask Jesus? How does Jesus respond?

____

____

What conclusion do they reach?

____

This trial opens at daybreak. This seems to be the formal appointment before the Sanhedrin. Only during the daylight is the Sanhedrin allowed to hear testimony and decide whether to put a man to death. The illegal hearings during the night need to be legitimized by this formal, daytime trial. Even though the end is a foregone conclusion, the leaders go ahead with the sham. With one accord, the Sanhedrin decides to put Jesus to death.

Politicians today are not the only ones concerned with their image. Jesus is very popular among the Jewish people and the Sanhedrin knows that they must "spin" the arrest and death of Jesus very carefully in order to maintain order among the masses. They are more interested in their public image than in reflecting the image of God.

● When do you find your focus most easily straying from the internal to the external? What do you need to do to keep your focus fixed on Jesus?

____

____

____

Thus, the Jewish nation rejects its Messiah. A people who had lived in anticipation of a Savior for centuries doesn't recognize Him when He comes into their midst. May our hearts never be so blind.

---

1 Davis, p38
2 Coffman, *Matthew*, p451; *John*, p420

Shadow Of Accusation

Jesus must be tired as the long night before the members of the Sanhedrin comes to an end. Having been up all night, suffering through the agony of the blood-sweat, enduring the emotional brutality of betrayal, and having been physically tormented by the men who were supposed to receive Him with joy, Jesus' heart and body are bruised. His spirit and His love, however, remain committed to saving you. This week we will walk the streets of Jerusalem as Jesus passes from Jewish hands into the hands of the Romans.

Day 1

✔ Read Matthew 27:1-10.

What change of heart does Judas have? What prompts his regret?

____

____

● Why do you think Judas has a change of heart at this moment?

____

____

What does Judas do with the thirty silver coins? Why?

____

____

What confession does Judas make to the chief priests and elders? How do the chief priests and elders respond to Judas?

____

____

What quandary does the return of the money bring them? What do they decide to do with the money?

____

____

How does Judas die? See also Acts 1:18-19

____

Early in the morning after Jesus' arrest, Judas learns of Jesus' fate. The Sanhedrin has decided to put Him to death. It is unknown whether or not Judas expected this to be the outcome when he first approached the leaders with his offer to betray Jesus into their hands. However, once the finality of the sentence becomes evident, Judas is seized with remorse. We can imagine that he thinks back over the years he has walked with Jesus and realizes that, despite the fact that Jesus has not been the mighty political and military figure the people hoped He would be, this gentle man does not deserve death.

● Is there a difference between being "seized with remorse" and repentance? Explain.

____

____

Judas does not seem to repent here in the New Testament sense of the word. The English phrase translated as "seized with remorse" comes from the Greek word *metamellomai*, which means, "to care afterward."[1] The word "repent", as it is found in Acts 2:38 for example, is a different Greek word – *metanoia*, which means, "to think differently."[2] Repentance is more than being sorry about the consequences of our actions. Repentance should literally change our minds, reshape our hearts, and alter our behavior. It is not so much a feeling as a decision to reroute the direction of our lives.

Repentance is recognition of our need for God's grace and provides the motivation we need to come before Him in obedience and humility.

Read Acts 2:38. Why is repentance a necessary part of our salvation process?

____

____

Judas seems to be overcome with the emotion of remorse. As guilt wells up inside of him, he seeks to assuage his conscience by returning the money he had coveted only hours before. Since the formal meeting place for the Sanhedrin is just off the Court of Women on the temple grounds, it is logical to conclude that Judas approaches the chief priests and elders here. As eagerly as he had once come to betray Jesus, he now comes to relieve himself of the burden of guilt that weighs on his heart. As he hands over the coins, Judas admits his sin and testifies to Jesus' innocence.

The end of Mathew 27:4 is one of the coldest passages you will ever read. The true heart of Israel's spiritual leaders is revealed. *"What is that to us?" they replied. "That's your responsibility."* No mercy. No thirst for truth and justice. No desire to point the way to God. This is how far even those entrusted with God's Word can fall.

● How can the way we react to people and their life situations make a difference in their ability to seek and find God? What responsibility does this lay on you?

____

____

____

Frustrated at their indifference, Judas throws the money into the temple and leaves in despair. As the priests pick up the coins, the irony surrounding their actions can only make us shake our heads in wonder at man's hardheartedness and God's grace. They discuss the righteousness of using blood money in the holy temple. Men willing to suborn perjury and commit murder are unwilling to defile the temple with a questionable offering. May this kind of stench never rise from our hearts to our Father's throne.

● Read Matthew 23:23-24. How do Jesus' words to the Pharisees apply to you today?

____

____

____

Judas leaves the city and heads to a field west of Jerusalem where the Kidron and Hinnom valleys meet. The soil is soft and full of clay, which is why it is known as the potter's field. Sharp, ragged rocks jut up unevenly from the slippery ground.[3] Judas finds a sturdy looking tree and taking either his linen belt or another cord, wraps it around his neck, tying it to the tree branch. As he hangs himself from the tree, the branch evidently cannot hold his weight and he is dashed onto the jagged rocks below.

With Judas' money, the priests buy this potter's field for use as a cemetery for foreigners. It is given the name the Field of Blood and, unbeknownst to them, the priests fulfill another prophecy foretold by Zechariah. (Zechariah 11:12-13)

● What hope do you have that Judas does not have? In what way is hope the fuel that powers our ability to face tomorrow?

____

____

Day 2

Jesus is now led from the temple area that houses the chambers of the Sanhedrin to the residence of the Roman governor, Pontius Pilate. Here, as before the Jewish officials, Jesus will stand trial three times – two before Pilate and one before Herod. Since these two men play such a pivotal role in the death of our Lord, let's take this opportunity to meet them and catch a glimpse of their character.

Pontius Pilate

Very little is known about the man who plays such a central role in the death of Jesus. If not for his heinous decision, he would have faded into obscurity.

Look at the following Scriptures and glean what information you can about Pilate and his character.

John 18:28 ____

Matthew 27:19 ____

Mark 15:9-10 ____

Mark 15:15 ____

Luke 13:1 ____

Pontius Pilate is the fifth procurator or governor of Judea. He serves Rome in this capacity from 26-36 A.D. The Roman governor has his official headquarters in Caesarea on the coast of the Mediterranean Sea where the weather is moderated by the ocean breezes.[4] During times of national Jewish holidays, like Passover, Pilate considers it prudent to be in Jerusalem to maintain order among the frequently rebellious Jews. While in Jerusalem, Pilate and his wife, whose name based on tradition is Procula, stay in the luxurious palace of Herod just southwest of the Jewish temple.[5] This palace now takes on the title of the Praetorium which indicates that it is, at least for the duration of Pilate's visit to Jerusalem, the headquarters of the Roman government.[6] Soon the world's greatest drama will be played out on its steps.

As to Pilate's character, history confirms the glimpse we see in the Gospels. He is reported to be "merciless, cruel", and "noted for his habitual brutality."[7] Mark also gives us two other important insights into Pilate's heart. The first is found in Mark 15:9-10. Pilate, in his dialogue with the Jewish leaders, recognizes that they are handing Jesus over to him out of envy. This tells us that Pilate is politically astute. He is intelligent enough to see through the charade being played out by the chief priests and cynical enough to not be surprised by their political intrigue.

The second insight recorded by Mark is found in Mark 15:15. Here we see Pilate's downfall, his Achilles' heel. As we shall see as Jesus undergoes the trial, Pilate, from the beginning, is convinced of Jesus' innocence. But in choosing where to place his heart, he values what is popular over what is right.

● In what ways does our society make this a difficult choice?

____

____

● How do we train our children to choose God's path even at the expense of popularity and social acceptance?

____

____

According to outside historical records, Pilate displeases Emperor Tiberius and is exiled to Vienna where, according to tradition, he commits suicide in 41 A.D.[8]

Herod Antipas

The family of Herod is more intimately connected to our Lord than Pilate. Throughout His life, the hand of Herod's family reaches out and tries to touch Jesus. It is Herod Antipas' father, Herod the Great, that kills all the baby boys at the time of Jesus' birth to prevent the ascension of a new king. Though he only sees Jesus once, Herod too will have to make a choice about the kingdom of God.

Look at the following Scriptures and glean what information you can about Herod and his character.

Luke 3:1 ____

Matthew 14:1-11 ____

Mark 8:15 ____

Luke 3:19 ____

Upon the death of Herod the Great, his kingdom is divided into three parts to be ruled over by three of his sons. Herod Antipas is given the lands of Judea and Perea to rule. His official residence is in Tiberius on the Sea of Galilee but, like Pilate, his presence in Jerusalem during such an important time like Passover is considered crucial.[9] It is thought that Herod takes up residence in the palace once occupied by the Maccabees located near the home of the high priest.[10]

Like Pilate, we find Herod to be a man of exceedingly low morals. In addition to many other evils, Herod marries his brother's wife. John the Baptist rebukes him for his adultery and crudeness. Showing the hardness of his heart, Herod responds by putting John in prison. After watching a sensuous dance performed by his wife's daughter, Herod beheads John at the girl's request.

Later, we hear Jesus warning the disciples to be wary of the corrupt influence exerted by Herod. This tells us that Herod is well known throughout the region and that his sway in the area is strong.

An interesting aspect of Herod's character is revealed in Mark 6:20b. We are told, *"When Herod heard John, he was greatly puzzled; yet he liked to listen to him."* All of the truth and righteousness of God is laid out before him, and for Herod it is merely entertainment.

In what way does Herod's attitude echo that found in Ezekiel 33:30-32?

____

____

● What lesson does Ezekiel's message hold for you?

____

____

Day 3

✔ Read Luke 23:1-7.

Of what three charges do the Jews accuse Jesus?

____

____

Which charge does Pilate zero in on? Why?

____

Why does Jesus' answer cause Pilate to find Him innocent of the charges?

____

____

What charge do the Jews insist on promoting?

____

To whom does Pilate send Jesus? Why?

____

Luke is the only one who gives us this information about Jesus' first trial before Pilate and the audience before Herod. Arriving bound in front of the governor's Jerusalem residence, Jesus is accused of three crimes against Rome. First, Jesus is charged with subversion. Second, they claim that Jesus opposes paying taxes to Rome. Third, they argue that Jesus says that He is the Christ, a king. Let's look at each of these charges one by one.

Charge #1 – Subversion

What does it mean to be subversive?

____

What events in Jesus' ministry might the Jews misrepresent as evidence of subversion?

____

____

The Romans are extremely sensitive to the charge of subversion and insurrection. They want their hold on their empire to be absolute and do not tolerate those who would engage in rebellion against it. This then is the first charge that they level against Jesus. They claim that it is Jesus' intention to lead His followers in a revolt against Rome.

Contrary to their charge of rebellion and revolt, Jesus' followers are commanded to live a life of submission to government authorities.

● Read Romans 13:1-2. In what way does submitting oneself to governing authorities bring glory to God? How should this God-ordained submission affect the way we talk about and act toward our leaders?

____

____

____

On a more spiritual plane, one might argue that Jesus did not come to institute rebellion but to quash it. The majesty and authority of God is from everlasting to everlasting. Yet, there is one who has set himself up in defiance to God's eternal throne. It is this usurper that Jesus has come to ultimately defeat.

Read Ephesians 2:1-2 and John 12:31-32. Identify the rebel.

____

Charge #2 – Opposition to paying taxes

Why would opposition to paying taxes be considered serious enough to warrant death?

____

Jesus has already responded to this charge from the Jews in Matthew 22:15-22. What principle does Jesus lay out for us to follow?

____

In this passage, as well as Romans 13:6-7, Christians are clearly taught that paying taxes is not only our duty as citizens, but our responsibility as followers of Jesus. Refusing to pay taxes is its own kind of rebellion. Without the monetary means to carry out its responsibilities, a government will crumble. Since we are to live a life of submission to authority, we honor God when we pay the taxes necessary to support our government.

Of course, Jesus' teaching does not end there. While we are to render unto Caesar what is Caesar's, we are more importantly to give to God that which bears His image.

● In whose image are you made? Genesis 1:27 In what way do you seek to daily honor God with your life?

____

____

Charge #3 – Claims to be Christ, a king

In what way is this charge true? In what way is it false?

____

____

In this charge we find a picture of the kind of Messiah the Jewish people had come to expect. The people long for a leader that will equip them to rise up and throw the Roman beast off their backs. They yearn for the return of the time of David when Israel was strong, wealthy, and in submission to no one. They have idealized the Messiah as some kind of mighty warrior-king who would reestablish Jerusalem as an international power.

In fact, when the opportunity to be such a king was thrust upon Him, what did Jesus do?
John 6:15

____

The truth is that Jesus is indeed the Christ, the long-ago promised Messiah. The sorrow we find in this moment is that because He did not meet their expectations, they cast Him aside. They would rather have no king than accept one who does not match their vision.

● Are there ever times when our expectations and desires stand in conflict to the reality of Jesus? Explain.

____

____

● How do we learn to continually match our vision with His?

____

____

Day 4

After listening to the three charges outlined by the Jews, Pilate focuses in on only one point – *"Are you the king of the Jews?"* Jesus answers plainly and simply. *"Yes, it is as you say."* However, there is something about Jesus' answer that prompts Pilate to affirm His innocence. Whether it is Jesus' calm and direct answer that stands in contrast to the wild zealots that are regularly paraded before him or the political astuteness of a man who has ruled the Jews for years and knows well their intrigues, Pilate refuses their request in very short order.

The Jews, of course, are not satisfied. They have traveled far down this path. It is now or never. They raise their voices and insist that Jesus is stirring up large numbers of people all over Judea. He started in Galilee, they argue, but now His subversion extends to Jerusalem itself.

At the mention of Galilee, Pilate sees a political opportunity. His old enemy Herod is in town for the Passover. He can send the case over to him, be done with these bothersome Jews, and score a few political points on the side. Pilate seizes the opportunity. Jesus is sent before Herod.

✔ Read Luke 23:8-12.

Why is Herod pleased about seeing Jesus?

____

How does Jesus respond to Herod's curiosity? Why?

____

____

Describe what you think "vehemently accusing" means.

____

What does Herod do when he gets no response from Jesus?

____

____

What about this day do you think bridges the animosity between Herod and Pilate?

____

Sly, crafty Pilate sends the insistent Sanhedrin members to the house of Herod. Herod acknowledges the recognition of his jurisdictional authority and almost gleefully welcomes Jesus. He is thrilled to finally grant an audience to this most talked about man. He almost seems to expect some grand theatrical performance with a miracle as the highlight of the show.

As Herod begins to ply Jesus with questions, his high hopes sour in his mouth. Jesus refuses to answer. He will not play Herod's game. In the background we hear the chorus of accusations rising through the air. It seems the more insistent Herod's questions, the greater the vehemence spewed by the Jewish leaders.

Read Isaiah 53:7. What prophecy is Jesus fulfilling at this moment?

____

Remember, with one word, Jesus can call the legions from heaven and all of the abuse, insults, deception, and humiliation will be swept away. Except, if He does that, your sin will not be able to be washed away. So instead we see Jesus, obedient to His Father's will, silently enduring shame so that we may one day stand before Him unashamed.

● What strikes you most forcefully as you watch Jesus through these five trials? Where in your own life do you most need to emulate this quality of Jesus?

____

____

Finally, Herod realizes that he is not going to get the show he so eagerly desires. If Jesus will not perform for him, then he will entertain himself by using Jesus in his own way. Herod and his soldiers begin to mock and ridicule our Savior.

● In what way does the world mock and ridicule Jesus today?

____

____

● Have you ever been ridiculed because of the name of Christ? Explain.

____

____

Read Revelation 2:3,7. What awaits those who persevere and endure hardships for His name?

____

With mocking words still dripping from his lips, Herod lays an elegant robe across Jesus' shoulders and sends him back to seek judgment before Pilate.

In Herod, we see the unfortunate way many receive the Gospel of Jesus. They see the good news as they see any good story – entertaining but totally irrelevant to their everyday lives. They will endure, perhaps even seek out, the message as long as it brings chills of delight and doesn't step on their hearts and toes. But as soon as the novelty wears off, the ridicule begins. Ridicule and mockery allow one to hold the Gospel at arm's length. At arm's length, you don't have to look too closely at your sin.

The world is very good at mocking Christianity. Christians are made to feel guilty for being absolute when they teach about God's boundaries concerning morality and sexual purity. Followers of Jesus are made to feel out of step with the times when they insist that Jesus is The Way, the only Way, to reach heaven. Those who wear the name of Jesus are treated with contempt for donning the garments of honesty and integrity in a world enamored with ambition and power.

But don't let the world fool you. Underneath all of the mockery and ridicule are hearts aching with the pain of sin. Jesus saw it. He asks you to do the same. And then, once again, lead them to the shadow of the cross.

1   Strong, p839
2   Strong, p838
3   Edershiem, p575
4   *NIV Study Bible*, p1527
5   Edersheim, p566, 569
6   Edersheim, p566
7   Halley, p414
8   Lockyer, *All the Men of the Bible*, p278
9   *NIV Study Bible*, p1585
10   Edershiem, p572

Shadow Of Power

As Herod sends Him back to Pilate, Jesus knows the final judgment is near. Exhausted both physically and emotionally, Jesus' resolve remains true to His Father's purpose. This week we will watch with heavy hearts as Jesus, the Lamb of God, is condemned to die. Take a moment as you begin to ask God to help you see the lessons He has planned for you this week and once again praise Him for allowing you to stand in the shadow of the cross.

Day 1

✔ Read John 18:28-38.

What sign of hypocrisy do you see here among the Jews?

____

____

What reason do the Jews give for bringing Jesus to Pilate?

____

Why is it important that even the mode of His death be a fulfillment of prophecy?

____

____

● How does Jesus describe His kingdom? In what way are you a part of that kingdom?

____

____

For what reason has Jesus come into the world?

____

What question does Pilate ask Jesus? What judgment does he make?

____

As the Jews once again approach Pilate, we catch another glimpse of the spiritual blindness of these religious leaders. They are concerned about their ceremonial cleanness while trying to kill the Messiah! Talk about having your priorities mixed up. And yet, as I say this, I know that we, too, are guilty of majoring in the minors. Sometimes we get so focused on minutiae, on protecting our own comfort zone, that we cannot see that we have failed the Son of God.

● In what way can hypocrisy ruin our testimony about Jesus and His church?

____

____

● How do you guard against hypocrisy in your own life?

____

____

Pilate again tries to throw the ball back into the Jews' court. He tells them to try Jesus themselves — they don't need the Roman governor's involvement. Here again we see Pilate's insight into the situation. It is evidently clear that the dispute the Jewish leadership has with Jesus is religious in nature and falls far short of the accusations they have leveled against Him.

Finally, the truth starts to rise to the surface. The Jews want Jesus dead and have no authority to execute Him. They need Rome's help. The Jews cannot kill Jesus by themselves; thus, the Gentiles will bear some responsibility for His death as well. No one will be able to take sides and claim that the others alone caused His death.

Whether Jew or Gentile, each will carry part of the guilt so that all may participate in His grace.

Read Matthew 20:17-19 and John 3:14-15.

What kind of death does Jesus say He must die? Why?

____

____

The primary form of execution among the Jews is stoning. If the Jewish leadership had the authority to execute Jesus on their own, Jesus would never have died the kind of death that He foretold. It is important to see that what happens here in the heat of these next few minutes is not guided by the swirling emotions of men. God has planned for Jesus to die at this exact time and in this brutal manner to fulfill His good and perfect will. Even though, from a human perspective, it seems the hand of man is on the steering wheel, God is in control.

● When do you most need to be reminded that God is in control?

____

____

Pilate again asks Jesus about His identification as a king. Jesus not only affirms that He is a King, but lays out the nature of His kingdom to Pilate. His kingdom will not rise because of a physical battle, but will be founded on the spiritual victory that Jesus wins over sin and death. This is His purpose — the reason for which He was born. It is interesting that Jesus states that His entire life and ministry have been a testimony to the truth. Remember, He is standing trial before a Roman authority, yet His testimony goes far beyond this moment.

Examining each moment of His time on earth focuses the light of truth to shine on the goodness of God, the sinfulness of man, the love of Jesus, and the hatred of our enemy.

Pilate responds by asking, *"What is truth?"* We tend to think that moral relativism is a new phenomenon. It is not. Man has always wanted to see truth as flexible and individually adjustable. Our society screams that no one has the right to define truth for others. So I'll leave the question with you.

What is truth?

____

Actually, I'll have to admit to that being a bit of a trick question because if you ask the wrong question, you'll never get the right answer. You see, Pilate and our society have got it all wrong. The question isn't, "What is truth?" The question is, "Who is truth?"

Write John 14:6.

____

____

Day 2

✔ Read Matthew 27:15-20 and Luke 23:13-19.

What Passover custom comes into play during the trial of Jesus? Why does Pilate bring this custom up now?

____

Describe Barabbas.

____

Why does Pilate choose to place Barabbas and Jesus side by side?

____

____

What report does Pilate's wife send to him?

____

To what conclusion have both Pilate and Herod come?

____

How do the chief priests influence the people?

____

Having questioned Jesus, both Pilate and Herod come to the conclusion that Jesus is innocent of the charges made against Him. While Pilate repeatedly expresses this opinion to the Jews, their stubborn hearts will not listen to God or man. Intent upon killing Jesus, they continue to press Pilate for His execution.

At this Pilate employs another political tool in an attempt to release Jesus while pacifying the difficult Jewish leadership. Remember, the relationship between the Jews and Rome is strained at best and in an uproar most of the time. Peace in the region is extremely tenuous and governors are judged by the Emperor on how well they maintain control in their assigned areas. Pilate cannot afford to upset the Jews to the point of sparking a rebellion.

● In what way can being politically correct come into conflict with doing what is right?

____

____

As a token of consideration to the conquered nation, it has become the governor's custom to release a political prisoner as a symbol of goodwill. Pilate decides that the best avenue to free Jesus, and allow the Jewish leadership to maintain some dignity, will be to release Him as a gesture of friendship. Pilate decides to hold up the innocent Jesus beside a notorious prisoner named Barabbas. Surely, the people would want their Christ rather than a convicted felon.

Pilate has underestimated the Jewish leadership, however. Intensely focused on finding an avenue for Jesus' death, the chief priests and experts of the law shout for the prisoner Barabbas and rally the people to do the same.

Little is known about Barabbas but what we do see is not encouraging. Matthew tells us that he is notorious, while Luke tells us the specifics of his case. Barabbas is an insurrectionist who has committed murder while causing an uprising in the city. From this we can conclude that Barabbas is probably a member of the Zealots – a sect of the Jews intent on revolution against Rome.

In Barabbas, however, we have a startling picture. In many ways he encapsulates all that is wrong with the Jewish notion of the Messiah. As he stands next to Jesus, the Jewish nation has the opportunity to choose whom it will follow – a counterfeit savior or the genuine Christ.

● What kind of counterfeit "saviors" does the world offer today?

____

____

Let's look at four points of comparison between Jesus and Barabbas.

First, their names. Barabbas' name is Aramaic and means "son of abba" or "son of the father."[1]

Read Mark 14:36. How does Jesus address God His Father?

____

Jesus, too, is the Son of Abba or to state it differently, the Son of the Father. As Jesus is presented side by side with Barabbas, the Jews first choice is to choose between a son of this world or the Son of God. They must now choose a leader – one who will follow the worldly path or One who will lead them to heaven.

● How does Jesus call us to address God? Matthew 6:9 What privileges are inherent in doing so?

____

____

Second, their missions. Barabbas is in prison for being an insurrectionist. It is interesting that he is actually guilty of doing what Jesus is accused of doing. Barabbas has taken it as his mission to fight Rome as the enemy of Israel. He is involved in an uprising in the city of Jerusalem against Roman officials. He longs to throw off the Roman chains that bind Israel and keep her from being free.

Jesus, on the other hand, longs to free us from a different kind of enemy. He is not nearly as concerned with the political pressures that shape our physical lives as the sin that imprisons our souls.

Read Romans 6:16-18. Obedience clearly defines whom you serve. By observing your behavior, what can your neighbors, family, and friends determine about whom you serve?

____

____

Third, the fruit of their work. Barabbas, probably in the process of leading this insurrection, commits murder. He takes life and sacrifices it on the altar of his ideals. In contrast, we see Jesus coming to give life, not take it away.

Read John 10:10. In what way does Jesus contrast Himself with the thief?

____

● In what way are you living an abundant life because of Jesus? In what way have you thanked Him for that abundance?

____

____

Finally, the results. As we are introduced to Barabbas, we find him sitting in jail and facing death. He is defeated. He has not and cannot accomplish his goal. He is unable to save himself or his nation. Jesus, we can say with joy, is on the verge of victory. By His death, He will not only provide salvation for this nation, but men of every nation.

It is not a random choice that the people face this day. It is the choice of a lifetime. The same choice is placed before you. Will you pick the counterfeit savior or choose to follow the genuine Christ?

Day 3

 Read John 19:1.

In what way does Pilate punish Jesus?

____

As the crowd cries for the release of Barabbas, Pilate's mind searches for another way to free Jesus. While it might not seem like justice to us, Pilate determines that perhaps if he punishes Jesus, the Jews will be satisfied and cease calling for His death.

Flogging, or scourging as it is sometimes called, was no light punishment. It was in fact called "the intermediate death."[2] It was a brutal, inhuman exercise in sadism. It was often used on prisoners condemned by Rome in order to hasten the death process. Many sentenced to be crucified didn't survive the beating.

Jesus is taken into the Praetorium by the Roman guards. (Mark 15:16) There He is stripped of His clothing and His arms are tied around a vertical beam, leaving His back exposed.

The instrument used in floggings is called flagrum. It is a short whip made of several cords of braided leather. Interwoven in these braided leather cords are iron balls and jagged pieces of bone. The Jews limited their floggings to 39 lashes, but the Romans had no such restriction.[3]

By Roman custom, two soldiers administer the beating. Each take aim at His back, buttocks, and legs. As they alternate striking Jesus with forceful blows, the iron balls cause deep bruises where they land. With the next blow, the sharp pieces of bone rip the skin open and the pooling blood is lost.[4] This is repeated over and over until the backside of Jesus' body is a mass of bloodied, ripped tissue and exposed bone.

The Gospels elaborate very little about the flogging of Jesus because the horrendous nature of this punishment was well known to the readers of the time. Eusebius, a third century historian, explains flogging like this, "The sufferer's veins were laid bare, and the very muscles, sinews, and bowels of the victim were open to exposure."[5]

Take a moment and listen to the taunts of the soldiers. Hear the sickening thud of the whip on His back. Lift your eyes and see the blood pooling at His feet.

Why does Jesus endure all of this pain?

____

Humble your heart. Let the price of your sin be embedded in your heart just as the lashes were embedded in His back. Resolve this day never to take His sacrifice for granted.

As they untie Jesus from the post, their cruel game is not through.

✔ Read Matthew 27:27-31 and John 19:2-3.

Make a list of all the abuse that is heaped on Jesus by the Roman soldiers.

____

____

____

As Jesus struggles with the immense pain and blood loss, the Roman soldiers set out to humiliate Him further. Across His raw and open wounds they drape a purple robe. Imagine the rough hands of the soldiers fixing that robe on His shoulders as the cloth sticks to the bloodied tissue. Next, a crown of thorns is roughly pushed onto His head. You have probably pricked your finger on a rose thorn before. You know how your skin jumps back from that pain. Now think how it feels to have many thorns pressing in on your scalp. Now they put a staff in His hand and kneel before Him, mocking and taunting Him. They can't imagine that this man now seemingly at their mercy could be any kind of king.

Their mockery becomes even more brutal as they take the staff from His hands and repeatedly hit Him in the head. They spit on Him (remember the open wounds) and slap His face. All of this is made more intense by the blood-sweat Jesus endured only a few hours earlier. The hematidrosis has made His skin very fragile and tender, increasing His suffering even more at this moment.

It is necessary to understand that Jesus' physical condition is quite serious at this point. The immense pain and the large amount of blood loss have compromised His circulatory system, and He is most likely on the verge of shock.[6]

 Read I Peter 2:21-24.

● What example does Jesus leave us? Why?

____

____

What response does He give to those who insulted Him?

____

To whom does Jesus entrust Himself?

____

Where does He bear our sins? Why?

____

● How are you healed by His stripes?

____

____

Day 4

✔ Read John 19:4-12.

List all of the ways in which Pilate tries to release Jesus.

____

____

How does the crowd react to seeing Jesus in the robe and crown of thorns?

____

Why do the Jews insist that Jesus must die?

____

Why does this make Pilate afraid?

____

● Where does Pilate's power come from? Why is it important that we understand this?

____

What statement do the people make? What is the significance of this threat?

____

Pilate once again attempts to placate the increasingly riotous Jews. He thinks that if he shows them the beaten and bruised Jesus they will be satisfied that He has been punished and let Him go. He brings Jesus out wearing the purple robe and the crown of thorns, but the crowd only grows more insistent for His death. *"Crucify! Crucify!"* they shout.

Pilate again refuses and tells the Jews to crucify Him themselves. This, of course, is impossible because the Jews are banned from carrying out such executions. The Jews respond by finally telling the truth. Their attempt to disguise Jesus as a revolutionary has failed. The truth comes tumbling out of their mouths as they adamantly explain that Jesus must die because He claims to be the Son of God. Jesus will die for who He is.

This news startles Pilate. As fear washes over him, he goes back inside the palace. He once again begins to question Jesus trying to determine the truth of this latest claim. Jesus gives him no answer. Frustrated, we see Pilate personally affronted by Jesus' silence. In his opinion, Jesus should be pleading with him and thanking him for his attempts to release Him. He demands that Jesus recognize the power that he holds over His life.

Jesus' answer is dramatic. He tells Pilate that the only power he has comes from above. Once again Jesus asserts that all things are within His Father's control.

● How can the illusion of power keep us from God?

____

____

Pilate returns to the Jews seeking a way to release this Man he knows to be innocent without compromising his position. The Jews seize on this facet of Pilate's character and run with it. They tell Pilate that he is no friend of Caesar if he allows this Man to go free. Here is Pilate's moment of truth – the cost of freeing Jesus will be the loss of his position and power.

● What has it cost you to follow Jesus? Seriously think here. What would you be willing to give up to wear the name of Christ – your family, friends, job, home? Consider Luke 14:26 before you answer.

____

____

✔ Read John 19:13-16 and Matthew 27:24-25.

What decision does Pilate finally make?

____

Who does the nation of Israel deny at this moment?

____

● What does Pilate do to publicly indicate his belief that Jesus is innocent? Do you think this absolves Pilate of guilt in the death of Jesus?

____

What responsibility do the people accept?

____

Pilate takes his official seat of judgment on the Stone Pavement. This is a raised stone platform that lifts Pilate above the crowd as he passes judgment. As Pilate presents Jesus to the people and says, *"Here is your king"*; the people cry, *"Crucify him!"*

What were these same people shouting only a few days earlier? Matthew 21:9

____

● How is it that our hearts can be so fickle?

____

In their insistence that Jesus is not their king, the Jews make an astonishing statement. They proclaim that Caesar is their king. Remember, the Jews hate the Romans. For any Jew to embrace Caesar as one with royal authority over them, worthy of their loyalty and honor is unheard of. Yet, this is how far they travel to kill the King of Kings.

How do God's words to Samuel in I Samuel 8:7 apply here?

____

● How do we daily acknowledge that Jesus is King of our lives?

____

Pilate, unable to muster the courage to set Jesus free, hands Him over to be crucified.

---

1 Lockyer, *All the Men of the Bible,* p66
2 Edershiem, p579
3 *NIV Study Bible,* p1528
4 Edwards; Gabel; Hosmer; *JAMA*
5 Strobel, p195
6 Edwards; Gabel; Hosmer; *JAMA*

Shadow Of Exhaustion

The last twelve hours have held unbelievable suffering for our Lord, and now as the dew dries from the grass and the sun fixes its place in the sky, Pilate caves in to the bloodthirsty mob and delivers Jesus into their murderous hands. Having been severely flogged, Jesus now faces even more agony. This week we will wince as the weight of the cross causes our Lord to stumble on the road and the ordeal of the crucifixion process begins. We will also have our faith reassured by the mighty evidence of God's almighty power.

Day 1

✔ Read Matthew 27:31, Luke 23:32, and John 19:16-17.

How do they prepare Jesus to go to His death?

____

Who takes charge of Jesus? What do they make Him carry?

____

Where is the crucifixion site? What is its Aramaic name?

____

How many others are led out with Jesus?

____

Taken away from the judgment seat of Pilate, Jesus is now turned over to a company of soldiers whose task it is to carry out executions. In deference to Jewish modesty, Jesus will be allowed to wear clothes as He is marched out to the crucifixion site. They strip the royal robe from His back. This is extremely painful as the robe, soaked with His blood, adheres to His open flesh. We can be certain that the hands of the Roman soldiers are not gentle as they pull the robe from His body, yanking on the ribbons of flesh laid bare by the whip. Jesus dresses once again in His simple, hand-woven garments.

Each condemned prisoner is assigned four soldiers who are responsible for carrying out the crucifixion process. The entire detachment is under the watchful eye of a Roman centurion.

As required of all condemned men, Jesus is forced to carry the instrument of His death. The cross beam of the cross is laid heavily on the blood-soaked shoulders of Jesus. It is rough wood, probably from an olive tree, about five to six feet in length, and weighing between 75 and 125 pounds. His arms are then tied to the beam with a cord to prevent Him from using it as a weapon against the soldiers.[1]

The execution site is known as the Place of the Skull. In Aramaic, it is called Golgotha; in Latin, Calvary. The actual location of the crucifixion site cannot be pinpointed with 100% certainty. There are, however, three parameters that help us narrow down its location.

According to the Law, where are executions required to take place? Numbers 15:35; Hebrews 13:12

____

What other landmarks must be close by the crucifixion site? John 19:20, 41

____

According to the Law of Moses, executions must take place outside the city. For an Israelite, this removal represents separation and banishment. While outside the city, we know that the crucifixion site is not far out in the countryside. The Roman purpose for crucifixion is not only punishment for the criminal, but to serve as a warning and a determent for the masses. The crucifixion site would be just outside the city wall in a conspicuous spot near a highway or main gate into the city.

The third parameter described in the Gospels is the site's proximity to a garden with tombs. With these boundaries in mind, scholars point to a hill just outside the Damascus Gate. Looking up, we can see a thirty-foot rock ledge that bears an uncanny resemblance to a human skull.[2]

To this hill of shame, Jesus' heart and feet are set. On Golgotha, Jesus will complete the task He came to earth to fulfill.

Write II Corinthians 5:21.

____

____

 Jesus, pure and innocent, willingly took all of the ugliness and filth of your sin and bore its fullest penalty so that you can stand whole – righteous before God.

This must be one of the most difficult moments for Jesus. Already in terrible pain, the weight of the cross crushing His swollen and bruised flesh, aware of the agony of the crucifixion awaiting Him, the physical trauma alone would break most men. Yet, even more than the bodily pain that He is enduring, is the weight of our sin being laid on His purity and innocence. The combination of physical torture and spiritual agony is staggering as He walks toward the shadow of the cross.

What difficult roads have you been required to walk in your life?

____

____

● What hope does Jesus' example give us as we navigate these difficult paths in life?

____

____

We have a Savior who sympathizes with our every tear and understands the pain of our most difficult journeys. He calls us to hold His hand, trust His love, and depend on His goodness to carry us through the dark circumstances of life.

As Jesus bears the wood upon which His body will be placed, another of His admonitions comes into focus.

✔ Read Luke 9:22-23.

What four things does Jesus require of those that would come after Him?

____

____

● What do you think it means to take up your cross daily? How do we do this?

____

____

____

It is here that we sometimes gather the mistaken picture that Christianity is a burdensome walk filled with drudgery, hardship, and trial, and the more serious the Christian, the more sour the expression.

Jesus, I believe, is painting an entirely different picture for His followers. Here we find the nuts and bolts of discipleship. *First*, we must have the desire to be a follower of Jesus. God will never make anyone follow Him against their will. Our hearts must be set toward seeking Him.

● How do we fan the flame of desire to seek Jesus in our own hearts? In the hearts of others?

____

____

Second, Jesus tells us that we must deny ourselves. Here, I think, is the most difficult step. We are called by Jesus to pass on what is pleasing to us and focus instead on what is pleasing to God. Living in a society that screams for instant gratification and worships that which pleases the senses, self-denial seems obsolete and futile.

● How do we train ourselves to seek what is pleasing to God?

____

____

Third, Jesus tells us that we must take up our cross. For Jesus, the cross is the physical reality of God's purpose for His life. For us, taking up our cross means to bind on our hearts God's purpose for our lives. Just as Jesus denied Himself and fulfilled His Father's will by dying on the cross for our sins, we must daily set our hearts in service to God's purpose for our lives.

● What is God's purpose for your life? How are you ensuring that you are daily serving God's purpose with your life?

____

____

Finally, we have words of great comfort and hope. Jesus tells us to follow Him. We do not walk alone. He leads the way, lights our path, and lifts our burdens onto His own shoulders. We are not called to go anywhere that Jesus has not already walked. He will guide us…home.

Day 2

As we watch the parade of soldiers and the condemned walking toward Golgotha through the streets of Jerusalem, we see the full weight of the night's torture come to bear on Jesus' exhausted body.

✔ Read Mark 15:21.

What man intersects with Jesus on the road to Golgotha? What are the names of his children? Where is he from?

____

What do the Roman soldiers require him to do? What can you conclude about Jesus' condition based on this fact?

____

On his way into the city, a man named Simon from Cyrene crosses paths with the prisoners on the way to their deaths. Little is known about the man forced to carry the cross of Jesus. Simon's hometown of Cyrene is an influential city in North Africa, west of Egypt, in what is present day Lybia.[3] There is a large Jewish population there and it may be that Simon is a Jewish pilgrim visiting Jerusalem for Passover. He is the father of two sons, Rufus and Alexander. There is a Rufus mentioned in Romans 16:13 and, while their mention by Mark raises the possibility that the two are well-known among local Christians, there is no way to be certain that this Rufus is the same man.

The fact that Simon is forced by the Roman soldiers to carry the cross at all tells us a great deal about Jesus. He is evidently so weak from the scourging and blood loss that He is unable to bear the weight of the seventy-five pound beam as He walks approximately one-third of a mile to the place of the Skull.

Doctors who have studied the medical aspects of Jesus' crucifixion agree that Jesus is in a state of hypovolemic shock at this point. This means that His circulatory system is in a state of shock as it struggles to deal with the large amount of blood He has already lost. This kind of shock causes His heart to beat very fast as it tries to pump enough blood through the body. He probably experiences a drop in blood pressure that can cause weakness or fainting. His renal system shuts down and He is extremely thirsty.[4]

Already in critical condition, the centurion recognizes that Jesus is unable to carry the cross all the way to the execution site. He searches through the crowd and focuses on Simon. Looking fit enough to carry the weight, this bystander is forced to carry the shameful burden for Jesus.

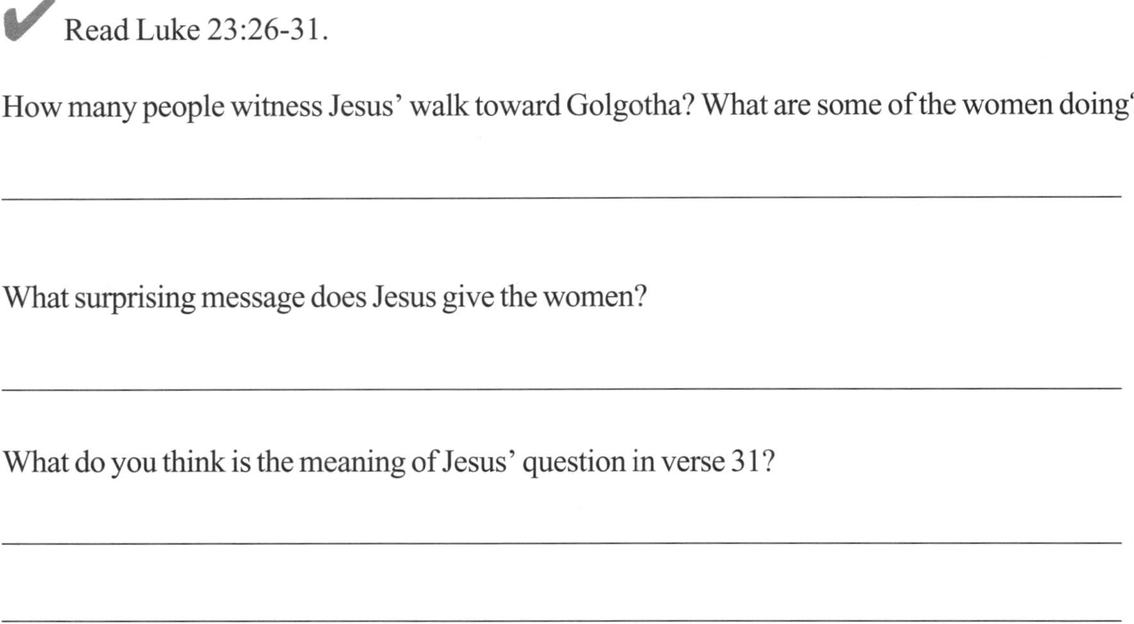

Read Luke 23:26-31.

How many people witness Jesus' walk toward Golgotha? What are some of the women doing?

____

What surprising message does Jesus give the women?

____

What do you think is the meaning of Jesus' question in verse 31?

____

____

It is shortly before nine o'clock in the morning and the streets of Jerusalem are bustling with activity. The sight of condemned prisoners draws a crowd as they wind their way through the streets of the city. Jesus' fame surely causes the crowd to swell even further. A group of women begin to wail and mourn for Jesus.

I stand in amazement at Jesus' response to their grief. As they grieve for Him, He grieves for them. Israel has rejected her Messiah. Jerusalem is murdering the Son of God. God's wrath will be poured out on them for what is happening this day.

Barrenness, always considered a curse by Jewish women, will be seen as a blessing in the time of the Lord's judgment. Of course, the annihilation of Jerusalem in 70 A.D. by the Roman general Titus saw the fulfillment of Jesus' words.

The women of Jerusalem are so caught up in the moment they don't understand the big picture. We need to be careful not to make the same mistake. As you watch Jesus struggle under the shadow of the cross and your heart grieves for His pain, you might be tempted to ask, "How could anyone do this to Him?" You need to be very mindful that it is for your sin that His blood drips to the ground. It is for your soul that He wrestles with death. It is for your salvation that His heart is pierced.

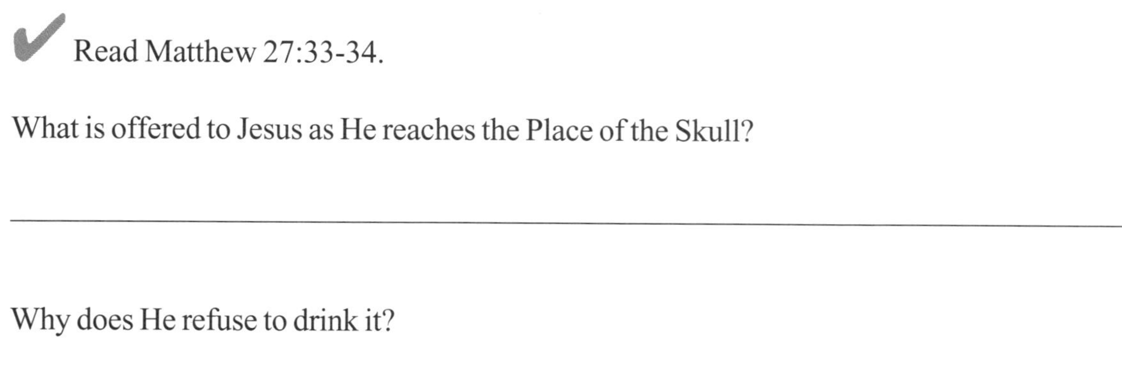

Read Matthew 27:33-34.

What is offered to Jesus as He reaches the Place of the Skull?

____

Why does He refuse to drink it?

____

Based on the teachings of Proverbs 31:6, it is the custom of a group of Israelites to show mercy to the condemned by offering them wine mixed with gall or myrrh. The mixture serves as a narcotic to relieve some of the horrible suffering of crucifixion. Jesus tastes the mixture but refuses to drink. The battle He faces requires presence of mind and steadfastness of spirit. His senses will not be dulled as He endures the suffering that pays the penalty for our sin.

Day 3

As we approach the mid-point of our study, it seems essential to take a step back and once again look at the whole picture of God's plan for our salvation. It is important to understand that the shadow of the cross does not first appear at the end of the Gospels. God had revealed the cost of our salvation long before Jesus ever came to earth as a man.

Read Revelation 13:8, I Peter 1:20, and Acts 2:23.

When did Jesus first see the shadow of the cross?

____

By what two things was Jesus handed over to be crucified?

____

● Why is it important to understand that the cross casts a shadow all the way back before the creation of the world?

____

____

In what way does God's set purpose and foreknowledge speak of His great love for you?

____

You are infinitely precious in the eyes of God. Creating you was for His glory and His good pleasure. Yet, even before He picked up the dust in His hand, God knew that sin would devastate the heart of His creation. So He planned and He prepared. He counted the cost and made man in spite of it. He knew the terrible price He would need to pay. That is how much He loves you. That is how much He longs to be close to you. That is how much He wants you to spend eternity with Him.

● In what way will catching a glimpse of God's great love for you change the way you walk with Him and talk with Him today?

____

____

Our God is so good! He doesn't ask us to base our faith on some mystical feel-good emotion but on the reality and historical truth that Jesus of Nazareth is the Son of God. He gives us layer after layer of proof so that our faith and trust in Him can rest on the solid foundation of His power and revelation. The world may assault us and doubt may attempt to erode our confidence, but God knew the struggles that we would face and has given us His Word that we may know the truth and see His eternal plan. Jesus Himself pointed to two important markers that testify to the authenticity of His claim that He is the Messiah.

Look at the Scriptures below and note these two markers.

John 10:38; 14:11 ____

Luke 24:44 ____

Independent of His teachings, the miracles that He performed demonstrate that His power and authority come directly from God. Secondly, the prophecies that fill the Old Testament directly point to Jesus as the promised Messiah. One of the truths with which we can cement our faith is the absolute fulfillment of the messianic prophecies in the person of Jesus Christ. There are literally hundreds of Old Testament prophecies that deal with everything from Jesus' ancestry to His second coming.

As we stand in the shadow of the cross, the prophecies about Jesus and the final hours surrounding His death are both pointed and specific. In fact, there are at least twenty-four prophecies about Jesus' betrayal, trial, crucifixion, death, and burial that come to fruition in a single twenty-four-hour period of time! These prophecies are written by several different inspired men five to ten centuries before the time of Christ.

Think for a moment about how amazing that is. David, who lived a thousand years before Jesus, was able by divine inspiration to give very specific and absolutely accurate information about the death of one of his own descendants. Yet, meteorologists today can't even tell us with certainty what the weather will be like tomorrow. What confidence our hearts can have in God! He holds the past and the future in His hands and tells us of His will and His plan so that we may rest assured in the love that purchased our salvation.

We will spend the rest of this week looking at these twenty-four prophecies that illuminate the path to the cross. Some of these prophecies we have already studied. Others will be examined in more detail later. However, it is both poignant and refreshing to look at this list in its entirety.

Prophecies concerning Jesus' betrayal

Look up the Scriptures listed below. Make a note of the prophecy and how it is fulfilled.

Prophecy   **Fulfillment**

Psalm 41:9   John 13:18-26 _______________________________________

Zechariah 11:12-13   Matthew 26:15 _______________________________________

                       Matthew 27:5 ____

                       Matthew 27:7 ____

Zechariah 13:7   Mark 14:27, 50 ______________________________________

Prophecies concerning Jesus' trials

Match the prophecy with its Old Testament and New Testament references.

		Prophecy	**Fulfillment**
____________	Accused by false witnesses	A. Psalm 22:7	1. Matthew 26:59-60
____________	Remained silent	B. Psalm 109:2	2. Matthew 26:67; 27:30
____________	Abused, beaten, and spit upon	C. Isaiah 50:6	3. Matthew 27:14
____________	Mocked	D. Isaiah 53:3 Psalm 118:22	4. Matthew 27:22-25
____________	Rejected by His own people	E. Isaiah 53:7	5. Matthew 27:31

● Why is it important to understand that Jesus is the fulfillment of all the Old Testament messianic prophecies? How will this understanding give you courage to share Jesus with a friend?

____

____

Day 4

Today we will continue our look at all of the specific prophecies surrounding the twenty-four hours of Jesus' betrayal and death.

● Why do you think that God gives us such a detailed picture of the death His Son would one day endure? What does He want you to understand?

____

____

____

Prophecies concerning Jesus' crucifixion and burial

There are fourteen prophecies that foretell about Jesus' agony on the cross, as well as the actions of those that move in the shadow of the cross.

As you look at each Old Testament prophecy, fill in the blanks that outline the specific detail about Jesus' death that God has revealed.

Prophecies that describe Jesus' physical state

________ Psalm 22:14 (NIV) "My ___________ has turned to _______________; it has

_______________ _______________ within me."

________ Psalm 22:16 (NIV) "… they have _____________ my _____________ and

my _______________."

________ Psalm 34:20 (NIV) "…he _______________ ________ his _______________,

not _______________ of them will be _______________."

Now match each prophecy above with its New Testament fulfillment listed below.

A. John 19:33   B. John 19:34   C. John 20:25

Prophecies concerning the words Jesus would speak from the cross

_________ Psalm 22:1 (NIV)   "My _________, _________ __________ why have you

__________________ _________?"

_________ Psalm 22:15 (NIV)   "…my _________ _________ to the ___________ of my

____________."

_________ Psalm 31:5 (NIV)   "____________ your _________ I ___________________

_________ ________________."

_________ Isaiah 53:12 (NIV) "…made ___________________ _________ __________

________________."

Now match each prophecy above with its New Testament fulfillment listed below.

A. Luke 23:34   B. Matthew 27:46   C. Luke 23:46   D. John 19:28

Prophecies about the actions of those in the shadow of the cross

_________ Psalm 22:7 (NIV)   "…they ____________ __________, ________________

their heads."

_________ Psalm 22:18 (NIV)   "…they _______________ my _______________ among

them and ___________ _________ for my _________"

_________ Psalm 38:11 (NIV)   "…my ________________ stay ____________

_________"

_________ Psalm 69:21 (NIV)   "…gave me ________________ for my ___________."

_________ Isaiah 53:9 (NIV)   "… assigned _________ ____________… with the

________________ in his death."

Now match each prophecy above with its New Testament fulfillment listed below.

A. Matt. 27:39   B. Matt. 27:57-60   C. Luke 23:49   D. John 19:23-24   E. John 19:29

Other prophecies surrounding the crucifixion

_______ Isaiah 53:12 (NIV)   "…numbered ___________   __________

___________________."

_______ Amos 8:9 (NIV)   "…the sun ________   _________   __________

______________ and ___________ the earth in

______________   _____________."

Now match each prophecy above with its New Testament fulfillment listed below.

A. Matthew 27:45   B. Mathew 27:38

Look back at your lists. God has given us amazing richness in both detail and scope of this twenty-four-hour period in the shadow of the cross. A complete chart outlining these twenty-four prophecies and their fulfillments can be found at the end of this book. Make a copy and put it in your Bible so that you can share the depth and breadth of God's eternal plan with others. When someone is struggling with doubt, it is often amazing to them to see the number of prophecies and specific details that God revealed hundreds of years before the time of Christ. There are three important reasons why He chose to give us this amazing insight.

First, the prophecies concerning the coming Messiah were given to prepare the heart of His people. For centuries, God outlined the specific nature of the promised Messiah – His birth, ministry, purpose, message, and, yes, His death. God gave them such a powerful view of the Messiah so that the people's heart would be overwhelmed with joy when Jesus actually walked among them.

Today, God longs to prepare our hearts for His presence as well. He wants us to study the details of His Word so that we, too, will be overwhelmed with joy when we recognize Him moving and working in our lives today.

● How has the study of God's Word prepared your heart more fully for His service?

____

____

Second, the prophecies concerning Jesus and His death speak to God's great plan. By laying out the specifics of these twenty-four hours with such detail, God leaves no doubt that it is He who is in control. The events of that day may well have left some asking, "Where is God?" God's answer to us on that day, and every day, is that He holds each moment in His hand and His plan will be worked out for His glory.

● How does studying these prophecies help you understand the plan that God has for your life?

____

____

Finally, God revealed these prophecies to men so that our faith can rest on the solid proof that Jesus is the Christ.

How did the apostle Paul use the Old Testament scriptures? Acts 17:2-3; 18:28

____

Jesus, by fulfilling in every way the myriad of prophecies laid out through the centuries in the Old Testament, provides an avenue for confident faith that He is the Son of God.

● In what ways does the world try to undermine the confidence of your faith? How does remembering the proof offered by fulfilled prophecy help to cement your heart in Him?

____

____

____

1 Edwards; Gabel; Hosmer; *JAMA*
2 Halley, p441
3 Coffman, *Luke*, p446
4 Strobel, p196

Shadow Of Love

We have reached the hill of Golgotha and now literally stand in the shadow of the cross. Jesus, exhausted, bloodied, weak from cruel torture, prepares to pay the final price for the salvation of your soul. This week you might be tempted to close your eyes to the pain and suffering inherent in the act of crucifixion. Instead, stand amazed at the heavy cost of sin, the cruelty of man to man, and the enormity of Jesus' love for you.

Day 1

Write John 19:18.

____

____

Within these few words lie a picture of horror and agony. To the first century reader, nothing else needed to be said. Crucifixion was a popular punishment used by the Romans throughout their empire. For many of the early readers of these Gospels, a simple trip outside their own city walls was all that was required to make the image of Jesus' crucifixion sear into their hearts.

Today, however, we are far removed from the awfulness of crucifixion. While executions are carried out in the United States, they carry none of the torture and suffering of these Roman death sentences. In order to fully understand the salvation that Jesus purchased for us on the cross, we must look unwaveringly at the price that He paid on that cross.

Crucifixion, as a method of execution, finds its origin among the ancient Phoenicians. Historical records tell of its use by Alexander the Great and the Persian kings, Cyrus and Darius.[1] As the Roman Empire grew and developed, so did the use of crucifixion as the preferred method of execution. The Romans developed a specific method for its use, including a set of rules for soldiers to follow when implementing the sentence. It seems the purpose of crucifixion was not just as a means of death, but as a mode of torture to exact as much pain and suffering as possible from its victims.

At the time of Jesus, Roman law exempted Roman citizens from death by crucifixion. Only slaves and the worst sort of criminals and rebels were made to suffer the indignities of the cross.

 Read Mark 15:25, 27.

At what time of day is Jesus crucified?

____

There are two other men crucified at the same time as Jesus. What is their crime?

____

How do these two men fulfill Jesus' words spoken in Luke 22:37?

____

As Jesus and the other two condemned men reach Golgotha, Mark tells us that it is the third hour. The Jewish method of reckoning time began at 6 AM. This tells us that our Lord was crucified at 9 AM in the morning. As the crowd reaches the execution site, Simon lays Jesus' crossbeam, or *patibulum* as it is called, down on the ground as the beams are untied from the arms of the two robbers. Rising toward the sky are three upright beams that will be joined with the crossbeams to form the cross. These upright posts, called *stipes,* are approximately 6-8 feet high and permanently fixed into the ground.[2]

What happens next is swift and cruel. Jesus is thrown on his back to the ground. Stripped of His garments, except a loin covering, the crossbeam is placed under his shoulders and a soldier stretches out His arm. Kneeling on the inner portion of His elbow, the soldier holds Jesus' forearm flat as the executioner approaches.[3] Holding the tools of his trade, the executioner takes out an iron spike, five to seven inches long, its body and head square in appearance. This he quickly drives between the two large bones in the wrist, approximately one inch below the palm of the hand. The soldier then extends the other arm, and this nail is forcefully driven in as well. Traditionally, the right hand is nailed first and then the left.[4]

Take a moment and find the hollow in your arm in the wrist area just below the palm. The main reason why this area is used, rather than the traditionally regarded palms, is because the palms of the hands are just not strong enough to hold the weight of a man to the cross. The weight of the victim would cause the flesh of the hands to rip and the individual would fall forward off the cross. By nailing the iron spike through the hollow in the wrist, the wrist's two large bones provide enough support to hold the man to the cross. In the language of Jesus' day, the wrists are considered to be part of the hands.[5]

What prophecy is partially fulfilled with this method of crucifixion? Psalm 34:20

____

Archeology has provided additional evidence of the method of crucifixion described in the Gospels. While in some parts of the empire Romans tied the condemned to crosses, archeological evidence has shown that in Palestine nailing was the preferred method. In 1968, archeologists in Jerusalem found the remains of a man who had been executed by the Romans in 70 A.D. Driven into his feet, they discovered a seven inch nail with bits of the olive wood cross still adhering to the iron and bones.[6]

God's Word will always be proved true! You can anchor your soul to the faithfulness of God and the integrity of His Word.

After Jesus' arms are nailed to the patibulum (crossbar), the soldiers then lift Him and the beam and attach it to the upright stiles. Imagine the immense pain as His body is jerked upward and His weight settles on the nails in His wrists. Once upright, the executioner nails His feet into the vertical beam. In order to position the body for the slowest possible death and maximum suffering, the knees are bent upward and the feet nailed to the cross. Traditionally, the right foot is placed over the left.[7]

As the sun takes its path through the morning sky, our Lord now hangs crucified on a Roman cross. As dreadful as these initial minutes are, the worst of the agony is still to come.

Write Psalm 22:16.

____

____

Day 2

More horrifying than watching the actual nailing of Jesus to the cross is the suffering and agony He endures as death approaches.

Read Hebrews 5:7-9.

Why does the Father hear the prayers of Jesus?

____

● Why is this heart attitude essential in our prayer life?

____

____

In what way does Jesus learn obedience from what He suffered? What is the result?

____

____

● Has God ever used suffering to teach you obedience? What was the result in your life?

____

____

The physical pain involved in crucifixion is pure agony. In fact, the pain is so extreme that the Romans coined a new word just to describe it – *excruciatus* that literally means "out of the cross." [8]

What English word do you see rooted in the Latin word above? Using a dictionary, write the meaning of this word.

____

Already in extreme pain because of the brutal flogging, Jesus' body endures new shockwaves of pain. As He is thrown to the ground to be nailed to the cross, the wounds on His back are once again ripped open and exposed to the dirt and any other matter laying in this area along this major thoroughfare. As the nails are driven into the wrist, they sever the median nerve, which sends lightening hot ribbons of pain shooting through His arms. Similar nerves are damaged in His feet, which make His nerves feel like they are on fire.[9]

The most wrenching pain, however, comes from the sheer act of breathing. As the weight of Jesus' body sinks down, the muscles become locked in an inhalation posture. This means that while He can breathe in, He cannot breathe out. In order to exhale, Jesus must use His legs and feet to push upward against the nails. Now He can take a few shallow breaths. This effort, however, causes a new wave of pain in the lower half of His body. Unable to maintain this position in the midst of such pain, His body once again slumps. Each time He rises and falls, the wood scraps His open, bloodied back spilling more precious blood.[10]

This is the agony of crucifixion. It is literally excruciating. Each attempt to raise the body to exhale requires extraordinary effort. As exhaustion sets in, death by asphyxiation or lack of oxygen often results. This anguish often lasts several hours with some victims surviving as long as three to four days.

Write Hebrews 2:9.

____

____

____

Jesus is our perfect example. Even though He is the Son of God, He was made to suffer and show Himself obedient. In all things and in all ways He showed Himself to be the perfect sacrifice for our sins. His perfection is proven true and pure in the fires of suffering. In this He qualified Himself to be our salvation. He remained sinless in the face of every human experience – pain, temptation, loneliness, betrayal, humiliation, and shame. As a result, God has crowned Him with glory and honor.

We must etch on our hearts here and now the suffering He obediently endured. The pain He endured should be your pain. The agony that enveloped Him should instead envelope you. He suffered your pain, paid your penalty, and bore death in His body to atone for your sin and to give you life, abundant and everlasting.

We will observe more of Jesus' suffering and pain as we stand in the shadow of the cross. As we close today, let's consider a statement made by the Apostle Paul and see if we can make it our own.

Read Philippians 3:10-11.

What five things does Paul desire in his spiritual walk?

____

____

● Which of these are easy for you to embrace? Which are difficult? Why?

____

____

How do we grow in our knowledge of Christ?

____

● In what way(s) does the power of His resurrection demonstrate itself in your life today?

____

____

● What does it mean to know *"the fellowship of sharing in his sufferings"* and *"becoming like him in his death?"*

____

____

● In what way does examining Paul's spiritual goals challenge you to examine your spiritual goals?

____

____

Here Paul makes a remarkable statement of faith. He longs to know Christ! Do you yearn to know Christ? Being an apostle, we might expect that Paul would already feel that he knows Jesus well. Instead we find that his heart longs to be even more intimate with the One who saved him so utterly. This should be our most fervent desire as well.

Next we see Paul longing to know and experience the power of the resurrection in his life. Notice this is more than knowing the resurrection story.

As a Christian, the power that God demonstrates at the resurrection is the same power that fills each day with hope and joy.

His power to raise Jesus from the dead is the power that transforms us daily into His image. It is the power of the Spirit bearing fruit in our hearts. It is the power unleashed by fervent prayer and selfless love. Don't let the world with its worries and cares unplug you from the power source that allows you to walk in the light.

In asking to know the fellowship of His suffering, we see Paul's maturity in Christ. We enjoy all of the blessings and joy that come with being a child of God. True spiritual maturity, however, shows itself in times of inconvenience, discomfort, and even suffering. It is one thing to walk after Jesus when things are easy. It is quite another to be challenged because of your faith — to be called to love someone who has hurt you or to serve someone undeserving. While few of us have had to experience physical pain for the name of Christ, we, like Paul, should long for our faith to be this strong and sure — this rooted in the love and person of Jesus Christ.

Don't settle for easy faith. Desire determined faith.

Day 3

As Jesus hangs on the cruel cross in excruciating pain, it would be enough just to gaze at Him in wonder and humility knowing that He chose this path for me. Instead we find that the hours that hold our Lord in deep agony also hold powerful lessons for us. We will watch as Jesus speaks and interacts with the people standing this day in the shadow of the cross. Despite His torment, Jesus speaks seven different times through the course of the six hours He is on the cross. Today we will look at His first words from the shadow of the cross.

 Read Luke 23:32-34.

Write Jesus' words in verse 34.

Of whom do you think He is speaking? What do they not understand?

____

____

● Remembering the inflicted agony we have discussed, how is Jesus able to forgive at this moment?

____

____

In what way is Jesus living out His own words in Matthew 5:44?

____

____

● What profound example is Jesus laying out for those who would be called by His Name?

____

____

Providing forgiveness for our sins is the primary reason Jesus came to this world in the form of a man, and it is this mission that we are reminded of with His very first words on the cross. While the other two men are probably screaming and pleading with the guards for mercy, Jesus intercedes with His Father for His executioners and pleads for mercy on their behalf.

As we hear Jesus utter these words, there are at least four important lessons that we can learn.

First, Jesus keeps His focus on His Father. Many times in the midst of great struggles and personal pain, it is easy for our eyes to fix on ourselves or the circumstances that are causing our suffering instead of staying fixed on the Father. We get wrapped up in the moment instead of wrapping ourselves more fully in His love.

● Of what do we rob ourselves when we focus on circumstances or people instead of the Father?

____

____

● In very practical terms, how can we learn to keep our focus on the Father in the midst of trying times and personal pain?

____

____

Second, we see Jesus, even in the midst of agony, clear and focused on the task God has given to Him to accomplish. It would have been so easy for Jesus to ask for justice rather than mercy. Isn't that what we often do? We want mercy for ourselves and justice for our enemies. Thank God that Jesus came to extend to us mercy and grace, and in doing so, took upon Himself the penalty of justice that we deserve.

● In what way does the world make it difficult to focus on the task God has given you to do?

____

____

● Becoming more like Jesus everyday is the task of each Christian. How do you seek to accomplish this task on a daily basis?

____

____

Third, we are given in Jesus' words a picture of His role between God and man.

What do you see Jesus doing at this moment?

____

✔ Read Hebrews 7:23-27 and I John 2:1-2.

What does Jesus always live to do?

____

● In what way is Jesus the perfect intercessor for our needs?

____

____

Why do we need someone to intercede for us?

____

____

What does His intercession allow us to do? Hebrews 4:14-16

____

____

Here we see Jesus standing before the Righteous Judge in our defense. We approach the presence of the Righteous Judge guilty and condemned by our sin. Jesus, as our Defender, pleads our case before the Father. He does not deny our guilt but rather, He asks the Judge to let Him absorb the punishment for our sin. We may freely enter into God's presence by the intercession of the blood of Jesus Christ. Because of His intercession, we can have boldness and confidence before the Father!

Finally, Jesus gives us a powerful example to emulate. Forgiveness is a benchmark characteristic of the redeemed. It is not an easy, superficial thing. Forgiveness is not an emotion but the actions of a heart and will that seek God's face. It requires a great deal of effort, trust, and faith to place the situation and person in the hands of God. Most of all, forgiveness is the action of a heart humbled by the knowledge that it has been forgiven much.

Write the last sentence of Colossians 3:13.

____

> When we focus on the Father, fix our minds on our God-given tasks, flood our hearts with the understanding that Jesus is interceding on our behalf, then forgiveness becomes possible.

Is there someone in your life who needs your forgiveness today? If so, use the space below to bring that person before your Father. Pour out your heart before Him. Ask Him for courage and strength to choose the path of forgiveness. If this is not your immediate need, read Colossians 3:12. Go into God's changing room and ask Him to fit you with whatever garment He finds lacking in your wardrobe. Pour out your request for fittings and alterations below.

____

____

____

Day 4

As we stand in the shadow of the cross and gaze at our crucified Lord, we realize that the image before us is more than physical. In the pages of the New Testament, crucifixion takes on a clearly spiritual dimension.

✔ Read Galatians 2:20.

● What does it mean to be crucified with Christ?

____

____

● In what way does Christ live in you? What freedom does this give you? What responsibilities?

____

____

____

Crucifixion is a symbol of death. Here Paul states that he has been crucified with Christ and that he no longer lives, but Christ lives in him. This is the essence of the transformation that takes place when we become Christians. This transformation carries us from the kingdom of darkness to the kingdom of Him who is dazzling light. We no longer live for ourselves; we live in and for Christ. Our daily walk of faith is cemented in the love and sacrifice of the Lamb, our King.

Paul, in another of his letters, gives us a thorough explanation of how this crucifixion of self takes place.

✔ Read Romans 6:2-11.

Where do we come into contact with the blood that Christ shed when He died?

____

Explain what happens during baptism as described in verse 4.

____

____

What hope is born in the waters of baptism?

____

From what are we freed when we crucify our old self with Christ?

____

Baptism is the critical juncture where a sin-encrusted soul meets the cleansing, redeeming blood of Jesus. It is in the waters of baptism that the old sin nature dies and a new person is born into the family of God. Just as we bury under the earth the physical body of death, so the sinful self is declared dead and buried in the waters of baptism. The person who steps into the water is full of sin, burdened by guilt, and subject to God's righteous judgment. As the person is immersed into the water this old self dies and a new creation is born, clean and pure because of the blood of Jesus. Just as Jesus was resurrected from the tomb of death never to die again, so this new person is resurrected in Christ and is given the gift of eternal life.

This new life has a new focus. No longer do we live to please our sinful nature. We live each moment to please the Father. We walk by faith and obedience as members of the kingdom of God. This message of hope and love we are to carry into a world that is dying.

Fill in the blanks below from Galatians 3:1b.

"Before your very ________________ ________________ ________________ was

clearly ________________ as ________________."

This is the message we are to take out into the world. While we have spent much time examining the horrors of crucifixion, we must never lose sight of the victory that Jesus gains for us on the cross. It is this anthem of victory that our hearts should sing everyday. Our lives should be a spotlight that leads people to stand in the shadow of the cross.

● How do you portray Jesus before the world?

____

____

● What do you need to do today so that the world more clearly sees the crucified Savior in your life?

____

____

____

Many people will read the book of your life long before they ever open the Bible. It is imperative that we not allow the pages of our life to be cluttered with the worries of living and worldly desires. We must have a determined focus that allows people to read the story of Jesus in our lives as they would the headline on a newspaper. Too often I fear we make it the fine print instead.

How do we develop this kind of focus? Again we turn to the heart of the Apostle Paul.

Write I Corinthians 2:2.

____

____

Read it again. This was Paul's focus – the only words on his page. He determined that *"Jesus Christ and him crucified"* would define every moment. What was the result? Because he allowed the power of God to be so evident in his life, God used him mightily to carry the message of the crucified Savior throughout the world.

● What do you think might happen at home, among your co-workers, with your friends, in your congregation if you resolved to have this same focus?

____

____

____

● Very practically, how do we go about making this focus our own?

____

____

Let the shadow of the cross fall heavily across the pages of your life. Proclaim its power with every breath. Resolve to focus on nothing less than Jesus Christ just as He resolved to do nothing less than be crucified for you.

1   Davis, p160
2   Edwards; Gabel; Hosmer; *JAMA*
3   Bishop, p489
4   Edersheim, 589
5   Strobel, p197
6   Strobel, p200
7   Bishop, p490
8   Edwards; Gabel; Hosmer; *JAMA*
9   Edwards; Gabel; Hosmer; *JAMA*
10   Edwards; Gabel; Hosmer; *JAMA*

Shadow Of Royalty

As Jesus hangs on the cross, the path for our salvation is being paved with His blood. He is opening the door to the kingdom for all who will come by obedience in His Name. At this moment, however, the work of salvation is not yet completed. This week we will stand in the shadow of the cross and observe our Lord as shame and rebuke pour from the lips of those He came to save.

Day 1

In addition to Jesus, there is another item nailed to the cross. It is officially called the *titulus* and is the sign on which the death charge is written.[1]

✔ Read John 19:19-22.

For what charge does Pilate declare that Jesus will die?

____

Why is the inscription on the sign widely read?

____

In what languages is the charge on the sign written?

____

Why do the Jewish leaders object to what is written?

____

Why does Pilate refuse to change the charge?

____

Where is the written charge finally hung? Matthew 27:37

____

The death of a criminal by crucifixion is meant not only to rid Rome of an enemy but also to serve as a warning to the general population to obey Rome or suffer the consequences. It is necessary, then, to inform the people of the reason that the criminal is being punished. For each condemned prisoner, a wooden placard is made that announces the crime for which he is sentenced to death. The sign is customarily carried in front of the prisoner through the streets on the journey to the execution site. The sign is then placed directly above the head of the crucified man. In this way everyone who passes by can understand the penalty for defying Rome.

As Jesus is being handed over to the soldiers to be taken away and crucified, Pilate orders just such a sign made. Written in Aramaic – one of the common languages of Israel, Latin – the official language of Rome, and Greek – a language widely recognized throughout the empire, the charge against Jesus is laid out – JESUS OF NAZARETH, THE KING OF THE JEWS.[2]

It is not clear why Pilate chooses to identify Jesus as the King of the Jews. It is doubtful that Pilate actually believes this accusation against Jesus that the Jews have brought before him. After questioning Jesus about this fact, he certainly doesn't consider Him a threat to the throne of Rome. It seems more likely that Pilate chooses this particular charge in order to embarrass the Jewish leadership. It is a way to twist the knife into the Jewish pride. Remember that the Jews hate Rome for its domination over their country. They long for a return to the glory days of David, when a Jewish king ruled over a Jewish nation. In their hatred and determination to see Jesus dead, the chief priests declare, *"We have no king but Caesar."* (John 19:15b) Pilate's charge seeks to insult the Jews by sarcastically reminding them of their vow of allegiance to Rome.[3]

The Jews are stunned when they learn of the charge written for all to see. This undermines their entire plot to curb Jesus' influence. As the throngs of Passover travelers clog the roads outside Jerusalem, they must have feared that word would spread like wildfire that the King of the Jews is being crucified by Rome. Instead of silencing Jesus and His followers, the chief priests seem to fear that Pilate's words will only lend credibility to Jesus' popularity. They bring their protests to Pilate who dismisses them without granting their request.[4]

Whatever Pilate's motivation is, what truth does the sign spell out?

____

 Read Revelation 19:11-16.

What four names are applied to Jesus in this passage?

____

____

Describe the rider on the white horse.

____

____

● In what way do you see the majesty of Jesus being displayed in this passage?

____

____

After reading Revelation 5:6-14, record the reactions of those who come into the presence of the Lamb.

____

____

● How do you react in the presence of the King? What can you learn from those in heaven?

____

____

Stop now and pay homage to the King of Kings.

Day 2

Before we leave this royal image of Jesus, we must take a moment and examine the privileges and responsibilities that come with being daughters of the King.

Write 2 Corinthians 6:18.

____

____

Royalty has always held a certain mystique for Americans. While politically we hold the idea of a king at arm's length, our culture seems in awe of those with the title of princess. We examine the way they dress, walk, and fix their hair. We secretly delight in their public foibles, and yet place them on a pedestal of dignity. Somehow princesses seem more graceful, more beautiful, more privileged than the rest of us.

The world's point of view, of course, only cheaply imitates the regal beauty God offers those who, by the blood of Jesus, are daughters of the King.

What kinds of garments adorn the daughters of the King? Isaiah 61:10; I Peter 3:3-4

____

____

● What difference do you notice between the way the world judges a princess' appearance and the way God looks at His daughters?

____

● How do we develop an appearance that is of great worth in God's sight?

____

____

More beautiful than the most famous fashion designer's gowns, God clothes us with garments of grace. Jesus' righteousness is the fabric from which our cloak of salvation is made. Imagine the dazzling light that radiates from the purity woven into each thread. Feel the softness of His love and the comfort of His peace. Of course, what makes these garments exquisite beyond our wildest dreams is the way these garments are prepared.

How are these garments prepared? Revelation 7:13-14

____

These beautiful garments of grace are not the only adornment of the daughter of the King.

What kind of fragrance does she wear? 2 Corinthians 2:14-16

____

How is this fragrance spread throughout the world?

____

● What is unusual about this special aroma?

____

● What do you think this means?

____

____

As Christians, we are to God the aroma of Christ being spread throughout the world as we daily live our lives honoring Him. It is a most precious fragrance. As we walk daily before Him, everyone we come into contact with is exposed to this beautiful aroma. The reaction to this amazing fragrance is varied — to some we are the smell of death. Have you ever thought of yourself that way? The smell of death is something from which we as humans recoil. That is exactly how some people will react when exposed to the aroma of Christ. As the fragrance of the knowledge of Him is absorbed, they come face to face with the truth that they are lost and death's prisoner. To others, the aroma of Christ that we carry with us is the fragrance of life. Just as we deeply inhale the scent of a beautiful flower or the aroma of baking bread, so those whose hearts love the Lord will embrace the aroma of Christ.

Note that those who incorporate the aroma of Christ into their hearts cause a very definitive reaction – whether positive or negative, there is a reaction.

● Think about the people that you have come into contact with over the last week. What kind of reaction did they have to the fragrance He spreads through your life? What does it mean if there was no reaction?

____

____

____

● What other privileges are granted to a daughter of the King? Which is your favorite?

____

____

The blessings and privileges that flow from being a child of the King are staggering. As a daughter of the King, I am allowed access into the presence of the King of Kings. I can present my requests and pour out my thanksgiving and praise before His throne. I am blessed over and over out of the exceeding abundance of His riches. I have a room in a mansion more beautiful than words can ever describe.

Of course, with great privilege comes great responsibility. There are many responsibilities that come with the multitude of blessings that surround a child of God, but in our focus on the majesty of Christ, one comes to the front.

Write 2 Corinthians 5:20.

____

____

What are the responsibilities of an ambassador?

____

____

What limitations are inherent in an ambassador's job?

____

What message has He sent you out into the world to proclaim?

____

● How would you rate your job performance as an ambassador of Christ? What can you do to improve yourself as a representative of Jesus?

____

____

____

Perhaps the most important function of a child of the King is as ambassador for His message. Each day we talk to people who need to know the wonder of His love and the healing that comes from His blood. God has placed upon His children the responsibility of carrying the Gospel to the world. Just like an earthly ambassador is scrutinized as a representative of his country, so we will be scrutinized by the world as representatives of the King. Every moment someone is paying attention to the message you are proclaiming with your actions, words, and choices. We need to be extremely mindful that our lives be consistent with the message we are sent out to proclaim.

Jesus left the throne of heaven to proclaim the establishment of an eternal kingdom and open the door for all to have a place within its borders. Along the way the King Himself is mocked, ridiculed, spat upon, and killed. Yet even in that moment, a man of paltry power named Pilate declared the truth – JESUS OF NAZARETH, KING OF THE JEWS — and on the cross that bore that sign, He granted us the privilege of becoming children of the King.

Day 3

As the soldiers settle down for the long wait at the foot of the crosses, we see them engaged in a very callous ritual – the division of the dying men's worldly goods.

 Read Mark 15:24 and John 19:23-24.

How many pieces of clothing does Jesus possess? Describe the unusual garment He wore.

____

How do the soldiers decide who gets the article?

____

● What significance do you find in the fact that these soldiers fulfilled prophecy?

____

____

It is a common practice throughout the Roman Empire for the possessions of the condemned to be spoils for the soldiers who draw the crucifixion assignment. The division of these meager goods takes on an air of crude partying as the soldiers gamble among themselves for possession of the garments.

Each Jewish man of Jesus' day regularly wore five pieces of clothing. They dressed in both an under tunic and an outer robe, a belt or girdle, sandals, and a head covering.[5] Since John tells us of five articles of clothing divided among the soldiers, it is reasonable to think these are the five items Jesus owned. The outer robe, belt, head covering, and sandals are all of about equal value.[6] Each soldier could have one piece, and Mark tells us that they cast lots, a rough form of gambling, to decide who gets what item. Jesus also owns an unusual piece of clothing, however. Unusual at least for someone so poor. He owns an undergarment or tunic that is completely seamless. This is a shirt-like garment that reaches down to the lower part of the leg.[7] It has been woven into its shape completely in one piece. The soldiers recognize the costly value of such a garment and agree to decide by lots who will possess the undergarment. Ripping the garment would make it worthless.

Casting lots is exactly what the soldiers do. Completely unknown to them, they are fulfilling an ancient Old Testament prophecy found in Psalm 22:18. Even here we see the hand of God. God used men who had no interest in or knowledge of Him to fulfill His purpose. Even here God is trying to reach His people with His love. As a crowd gathers in the shadow of the cross and watches the soldiers casting lots for Jesus' clothes, God is speaking to them through Scripture and proclaiming the truth of the promised Messiah.

● Has there ever been an unusual situation or method that God has used to reach your heart? Describe that time.

____

____

> God longs for your heart to have its total focus on Him. He has ordered His world so that you will be reminded of His greatness at every hour of the day. The dew on the flower petal, the warmth of the afternoon sun, the snow gleaming on a hilltop, the artist strokes of the sunset are all messages from the Father who loves you.

● How do we train ourselves to pay attention to the little taps on the shoulder God sends our way?

____

____

____

I cannot begin to tell you of the number of ways I have heard God's whisper calling me to bow my heart once again before Him. I have heard Him calling through the words of a song, the voice of a friend, the questions of my children, the solid faith of my husband. I have learned to listen to His lessons through my tears, while washing dishes and doing laundry, during times of illness and stress, quietness and peace. When my heart wanders too far from its focus on Him, He allows situations to develop in my life that force me to go to my knees and seek His face. Ask Him for open eyes and a listening heart. You will be amazed at the ways that God finds to remind you of His great love for you.

Our lessons from the unusual garment of Christ continue. The seamless tunic of Christ echoes a garment described by God to Moses.

Read John 19:23 again and describe the garment worn by Jesus.

____

Now read Exodus 28:3-4. What garment do you see in this list that is similar to the one worn by Jesus? For whom are these garments being made?

____

One of the garments God commanded the high priest to wear was a woven tunic. This garment was a seamless woven garment that was pulled over the head and worn by the high priest under the ephod and breastplate.[8] The woven robe Jesus wore is remarkably similar to a priestly garment!

✔ Read Hebrews 2:17-18.

What did Jesus become for us? What does this mean?

____

____

What does it mean, *"he had to be made like his brothers?"*

____

____

What is Jesus able to do on our behalf?

____

____

In the seamless garment worn by Jesus, we see a shadow of the priestly office in which Jesus serves on our behalf. The role of the high priest in the Old Testament was to make intercession for the people before God, to teach the people of God's ways and His commands, to offer sacrifices to God to atone for the people's sins, and to, once a year, approach the presence of God in the Holy of Holies on behalf of a penitent and thankful nation.

Jesus, as our High Priest, does all of these things and even more for us as well. He stands before the throne of God and makes intercession for us to the Father. He teaches us of His ways through His Word. His Spirit works in our hearts to transform us into the image of our Savior. He, Himself, became the perfect sacrifice that, once and for all, atones for our sins. Unlike the priests of old, however, Jesus continually sits *"at the right hand of the throne of the Majesty in heaven"* (Hebrews 8:1) and ushers us into the presence of God as well.

Not only is Jesus our High Priest, He grants us a special privilege as well.

How are you described in I Peter 2:4-5?

____

What are you to offer to God through Jesus?

____

● What kinds of spiritual sacrifices are you offering to God?

____

____

Write I Peter 2:7a.

____

Being able to offer our spiritual sacrifice to God is an amazing thing. As Christians, we are being transformed as God builds us into a spiritual house built on the Living Stone. As holy priests who daily serve our Lord, our very lives become fragrant offerings before God. We tend to view sacrifice in grand and noble terms. Here we learn that every action, when laid at God's feet through the blood of Jesus, can be a pleasing sacrifice. Whether you are changing diapers, helping the elderly, preparing a casserole, or listening to a teen's woes; by laying your whole life at the feet of Jesus, everything you do in His name is precious. Spiritual sacrifices are not about grandness of scale but about absolute devotion no matter the size of the task.

Take this opportunity to tell Jesus, the living Stone, how precious He is to you.

Day 4

Do you ever think of yourself standing in the shadow of the cross? Painters often visualize this scene as solitary and desolate. The truth is far different. The execution site is on a crowded road teeming with people intent on visiting the holy city for Passover. At the cross itself we find a wide and varied group of people, each of whom holds a lesson for us.

 Read Matthew 27:39-43 and Luke 23:35-37.

Make a list of the people standing in the shadow of the cross.

____

____

Without writing down the actual words that they spoke, make a note of the way that each group speaks to Jesus.

____

____

____

● What power do our words hold?

____

____

There are, at this moment, three different groups of people that the Scriptures focus our attention on – those passing by, the chief priests and teachers of the law, and the soldiers.

Those Passing By

Write down what those passing by said to Jesus.

____

____

What attitude or motivation do those passing by display?

____

What basic misunderstanding about Jesus' purpose and ministry do their words reveal?

____

____

Here the heart of Israel is revealed. As Jesus hangs in agony on the cross, the words of His chosen people become weapons against their Messiah. He has spent three and a half years teaching them about the coming of the kingdom of God. He has healed their sick, fed their bodies, cast out their demons, and raised their dead. Still their hearts are unmoved, their eyes unopened.

Evidently Jesus' words about rebuilding the temple in three days have been widely reported. Of course, Jesus is referring to His body and not the physical temple site, but that is exactly the point the Israelites do not want to hear. Jesus points the way to a time when worship will not be confined to a physical location, but where God will make the heart the temple for His presence. Their great pride in their glorious temple prevents them from seeing the greater radiance God has planned for all who will choose to be His people.

● Does pride ever prevent us from seeing the truth of God's Word? Explain.

____

____

Their next statement holds the greatest of ironies. They tell Jesus to save Himself. He does, of course, have the power to do this, but in order to save Himself, He has to give up on saving them and you. I stand in awe at the focus and self-control Jesus displays at this moment. He chooses to save you not Himself.

It is precisely because He is the Son of God that He cannot come down from the cross. To do so would mean that you could never go up to heaven.

The Chief Priests, Teachers of Law, and Elders

Summarize the way the rulers of Israel mocked Jesus.

____

____

What attitude or motivation do these chief priests and elders display?

____

It is almost astounding to see the chief priests, teachers of the law, and the elders of the people of Israel in the shadow of the cross at all. Having accomplished their purpose before Pilate, one would think they would retire and enjoy their "victory." Instead we see the hatred and insecurity of their hearts revealed.

Can you hear the gloating and mockery in their voices? Afraid that the sign Pilate placed upon the cross would influence the people, these leaders of Israel take up stations around the cross hoping that their derision will keep people from pondering why this man was named by Rome as King of the Jews.

Here are men so entrenched in their positions that they have burned the bridge that would allow them to accept Jesus as the promised Messiah.

● Are there people today who hold such positions? Explain. How do you attempt to reach such people for Christ?

____

____

● Examine your own heart. Is it possible that there is a piece of your heart that you are holding back from the authority of God? Explain.

____

____

The Soldiers

What do the soldiers offer Jesus? What does this tell you about their activities?

____

What mocking statement do the soldiers make to Jesus?

____

What truth about the kingdom of God do they not yet understand?

____

We have already seen the soldiers gambling to divide the clothing of the condemned among themselves. Now we see them join the crowd in mocking Jesus. They offer Him some wine vinegar, which is a sour wine drawn as a drink ration for all the soldiers. Here we see men so focused on worldly concerns that their minds are dulled to the importance of the moment taking place around them. When they become bored with their tasks, mocking Christ becomes a form of entertainment. They have no comprehension that the Man they jeer is not only King of the Jews, but of all the world.

● Do we ever become so caught up in our daily lives that we miss the point of being a Christian? Explain.

____

____

____

Next week we will spend time looking at the two men crucified with Jesus and their interaction with our Master. As we close this week let us remember with solemn hearts that the pain He bore for our sins was not just physical. Let us make sure that the attitudes of our hearts and the words of our mouth bring Him praise not pain.

1   Edwards; Gabel; Hosmer; *JAMA*
2   *NIV Study Bible,* p1634
3   Coffman, *John*, p439-440
4   Coffman, *John*, p439-440
5   Coffman, *Luke*, p449
6   Edersheim, p592
7   *NIV Study Bible,* p1634-35
8   Edersheim, p592

Shadow Of Mercy

This week we continue to stand in the shadow of the cross. We will watch as our Savior bestows mercy and grace on one of those condemned to die with Him. Our hearts will overflow as we see Him tenderly speaking to those He deeply loves. Expect to see amazing things this week. Ask God to open your eyes and your heart to His profound power and priceless love.

Day 1

Isn't our God great? I am deeply humbled and moved to awe and praise as I deeply drink from His Word and seek His face in the shadow of the cross. We must never lose sight that this is the place where we must root every moment of our lives. We should long for each day to be spent by His side, our hearts bound closely to His. All the hope, joy, peace, and blessings that flow into our lives because of His love find their foundation in what He did for us on the cross.

Write the words of the song recorded in Revelation 5:12.

____

____

____

If you have not had the opportunity today to worship the Lamb, please take the next few minutes to focus on Jesus. Let praise and thanksgiving pour out of your heart to the One who has saved you by His power. Use the words of heaven's song as a jumping off point.

Now let's go back to the shadow of the cross and watch as the taunts of His accusers fade into the background and one who is nearby is allowed the privilege of experiencing His mercy.

 Read Matthew 27:44.

Why do you think that men enduring the same punishment as Jesus would choose to insult Him?

____

Here is perhaps the strangest sight of all. The Gospels record that the two men crucified on either side of Jesus join in the abuse and insults being heaped upon our Lord. Perhaps they believe that if they join in the reviling of Jesus they will receive mercy from the crowd. Here we see the utterly hopeless placing their faith in the whims of a bloodthirsty crowd rather than in the One who is hope. Soon we will see that one of these men has a change of heart, but at this moment they are seeking deliverance from man rather than God.

● What kinds of things or people do we sometimes look to for deliverance from our problems?

____

____

● How can the desire to be accepted and fit in cause us to turn our focus away from Christ?

____

____

● How can the words of Hebrews 12:2-3 help us choose God's path rather than that of the world? Where in your life do you specifically need to apply this focus?

____

____

____

● How does the way that Jesus faced the cross help you face the trials and struggles you are dealing with in your life right now?

____

____

____

> Jesus' example is our hope! If we let Him, God can use each moment of our lives to shape us a little bit more into the image of Christ. Don't give up. Don't get discouraged. Give each piece of your heart to God and ask Him to recreate the beauty of Jesus in your life.

Read Luke 23:39-43.

What does the first criminal want from Jesus?

____

How does the second criminal answer him? How does he contrast the rightness of their sentence with the punishment of Jesus?

____

____

What attitude do you see in the second criminal's heart?

____

What request does he make of Jesus? What do you think this means?

____

____

What is unusual about his request?

____

How does Jesus respond? What do you think this means?

____

____

Now we hear the second statement that Jesus makes from the cross. As the morning hours have crawled across the sky, the excruciating pain Jesus endures has been compounded by the verbal abuse He receives from those around the cross. In at least one of those who have watched this drama unfold, we see a change, a softening of the heart. Jesus, as He always will when a heart reaches out for Him, responds with mercy and love.

As we have already noted from other Gospel accounts, it seems that both men, at some point, heap abuse on our Lord. Luke records the continuing insults of one of these men for us. His comments show us the true nature of his heart. He cares only about himself and what Jesus can do for him. He longs to be saved physically without thought of salvation for his soul.

● Do we ever fall into this trap? Explain.

____

____

This man represents the way many people approach Christianity. They cry for help with their immediate needs, but as soon as the need is past, they return to a life without thought of the Lord – until the next crisis.

Jesus longs for us to give our whole hearts to Him. While His blessings do fill our lives, He does not promise that in following Him we will be free of problems or that our lives will face no struggles. Rather, He does promise us His grace and love to deal with the inevitable pressures of this life so that our hearts will learn to depend on Him. His primary goal is the salvation of our souls. He wants you to spend eternity with Him!

● How can 2 Corinthians 4:17-18 help us withstand the pressures of this life and keep our eyes on our heavenly home?

____

____

Day 2

As we go back to the cross, we hear the second criminal rebuke the other criminal. What causes this dramatic shift? We have no information about this man other than these few words right here. We don't know if he ever heard Jesus preach or had any knowledge of the miracles He performed. What we do know is that he has been in the presence of Jesus for the hours they have hung together on the cross. There must have been something about Jesus that causes his heart to reexamine the taunts being thrown at Him. As unusual as it may seem, even the way that Jesus is dying speaks of His majesty and purity.

Write the robber's words in Luke 23:40-41.

____

____

____

The robber we hear at this moment makes three important points to the other condemned man.

First, he correctly notes that the other man does not fear God. Somewhere in those hours as he hangs on the cross and faces his death, this man begins to understand what it means to fear God.

● What does it mean to fear God? Why is it essential to do so?

____

____

✔ Read Isaiah 33:6.

Of what kind of treasure does Isaiah speak?

____

● How is it that the fear of the Lord is the key to this treasure?

____

____

How will the Lord respond to the heart that fears Him? Psalm 147:11

____

The fear of the Lord is a powerful turning point for our hearts. When we catch a glimpse of His majesty, power, and glory, our hearts learn to fear God and behold Him with awe. This fear isn't terror or being scared, but rather a recognition and deep respect for His holiness. It is literally standing in awe of our awesome God!

● How does Proverbs 14:27 describe the fear of the Lord? How do you see this truth worked out in the thief on the cross? In your own life?

____

____

____

Second, the robber points out the justice of the sentence these two men are under. In this moment, this man speaks for us all. He tells his comrade that they are being justly punished. They deserve death for their actions. Likewise, without Christ, we stand as equally condemned as those two robbers on the cross. Our actions and deeds provide testimony to the sin that resides within our hearts.

Look at Romans 3:23 and 6:23 and note what verdict the Righteous Judge has rendered in your case.

____

● How are learning to fear the Lord and the recognition of our guilt connected in the growth of our faith?

____

____

As we become aware of God's great holiness and our hearts are learning to stand in awe of Him, we also become uncomfortably aware of our own unworthiness and sinfulness. It is a terrible weight on our souls to realize our guilt and know that hope is blotted out by the blackness of sin. It is here that we most clearly see our need.

Third, this robber who hangs beside Jesus speaks a truth that no one during the last twelve hours would dare to say. This condemned man announces Jesus' innocence. Remember where this man is – dying on a cross, each word agony, the leaders of Israel clearly arrayed against Jesus, even the soldiers mocking Him – and this man chooses to speak the truth. It is in this truth that we have hope.

Write 2 Corinthians 5:21.

____

____

He died that we might live. He bore our sin so that we might wear His righteousness.

The robber then makes a remarkable statement of faith. He asks Jesus to remember him when He comes into His kingdom. This is absolutely amazing! The disciples have deserted Him, the leadership of Israel has crucified Him, but this dying man recognizes the kingdom of God. He doesn't ask for immediate deliverance. He asks for a place in the kingdom.

Jesus taught his disciples to pray in Matthew 6:9-13. What similar request does Jesus tell those who would pray in His Name to make?

____

While the kingdom of God has been firmly established, He longs for you to ask Him for a place in the kingdom. He has paid the price for your admittance. He has reserved a place of honor for you at the banquet table of the King. He will even clothe you with His robes of righteousness. All you have to do is ask to be admitted!

Jesus recognizes the faith that supports this man's request and responds with mercy and love. He tells the robber that this very day he will be with Him in paradise. The word for paradise has its origins in the Persian word for garden. It is only used two other times in the New Testament – once by Paul in 2 Corinthians 12:4 when he speaks of being caught up in the third heaven and again in Revelation 2:7.[1]

What promise does Jesus make to him that overcomes? Revelation 2:7

____

Jesus gives the thief on the cross grace and mercy and peace for his soul. While the manner in which he receives these gifts differs from the way Jesus bestows them today, these are the same things that Jesus desires to bless your heart with as well. The robber hanging on a cross beside Jesus teaches us the kind of heart we need to have to approach God. Today Jesus calls us to come to Him in obedience through baptism (remember the thief died two months before Pentecost!), and with us He wants us to bring a heart that holds Him in awe and recognizes its own unworthiness and Jesus' perfection. When we do, He gives us the sure hope of being with Him in Paradise!

Day 3

Today our attention shifts to another group of people that come to stand in the shadow of the cross. Watch carefully as Jesus' love overflows into provision for those dear to His heart.

✔ Read John 19:25-27.

Which five people do we now see standing in the shadow of the cross?

____

To whom does Jesus entrust His mother? Why does He make this provision?

____

____

What does John do?

____

Finally we catch sight of some people who truly love Jesus. As time passes and the agony increases, Jesus fixes His eyes on the woman who first held His human form in her arms. While Jesus is in agony, we can only imagine that Mary's heart holds its own agony. Any mother's heart would break seeing her beloved son treated so cruelly. At her side, we see his mother's sister, Mary the wife of Clopas, and Mary Magdalene. Accompanying the women is Jesus' beloved disciple, John.

We are first introduced to Mary when she is but a young, unmarried girl. God sends the angel Gabriel to Mary to tell her that she has been chosen to give birth to the Messiah, God's only Son. In an amazing testimony of faith, Mary responds with humility and places herself in the hands of God as His servant.

As the birth of God's Son takes place in the city of Bethlehem, shepherds in the fields witness the rejoicing of heaven as man's salvation takes human form. Angels invite them to behold the glory of heaven lying in a manger, and the shepherds leave their sheep to seek out the Lamb of God.

As the couple goes to the temple to offer the appropriate sacrifices after Jesus' birth, a devout man named Simeon meets them in the temple courts. Having prayed to see with his own eyes God's salvation, Simeon glorifies God and reveals to Mary an unusual prophecy.

Read Luke 2:34-35. What does Simeon reveal to Mary about Jesus? About her own heart?

____

____

____

Surely these words must have echoed in Mary's mind as she gazes at her son's tortured body.

Jesus looks at the mother He loves and the disciple that has stood so faithfully by His side, and, in an economy of words, gives the care of His mother over to John. This is the third of His seven statements from the cross.

● What do you think God wants us to take away from this tender moment between Mary and Jesus?

____

____

The Holy Spirit is an amazing writer. There are so many details about this day that I would like to know, but He chooses to reveal to us only those things that are important for the strengthening of our faith and the deepening of our relationship with Him. With this thought in mind, I do not believe that there are any insignificant moments recorded for us in God's Word. Each is written for our edification and growth.

Here, I think it is easy for our hearts to relate to this precious moment between Jesus and His mother, but it is not as easy to recognize that, in His example, there are spiritual lessons for us to learn.

The *first* lesson comes in the form of a reminder. As we stand two thousand years removed from the crucifixion of Jesus, we often view His death as an entirely divine moment. This interaction between Jesus and Mary helps us to remember Jesus' humanity. We cannot understand how it was possible for Jesus to be both fully God and fully man, yet we believe this truth. To focus on one at the expense of the other limits our understanding of what He did on our behalf. The Jesus we see in this moment has a family, a mother who grieves for her Son. He is fully human and His heart hurts for those He leaves behind.

Why was it necessary for Jesus to take on the form a man? Hebrews 2:14-15

____

____

Second, we see Jesus being obedient to the Law of Moses. We are told that Jesus came to fulfill the Law (Matthew 5:17) and we see Him doing this even from the shadow of the cross.

Look at the Ten Commandments listed in Exodus 20:1-17. What command do you see Jesus fulfilling at this moment?

____

● Following Jesus' example, how do you honor your parents?

____

____

Finally, we see Jesus providing for Mary's needs. Isn't this, at its most basic, the message of the Gospel. We need. We cannot meet that need ourselves so He makes provision for us. Even here in the deepest of pain, Jesus seeks to provide the emotional and physical support for His mother's needs.

● What has Jesus provided for you?

____

____

Sometimes in meeting the needs of His spiritual family, He calls others to meet their needs. He calls upon John to take care of His mother's needs. In the same way, Jesus calls us to tend to the needs of our brothers and sisters in Christ.

● In what way can you be God's instrument in meeting someone's need this week?

____

____

Day 4

We will spend the rest of our time together this week looking at the other three women present with Mary in the shadow of the cross.

From John 19:25, write the names of the three women with Mary near the cross, each on a different line. Now looking at Matthew 27:56 and Mark 15:40, write what additional information you glean about these women.

____

____

____

It seems that after the conversation between Jesus and Mary, we later find the women some distance from the cross. Here we are able to gather a little bit more information about these women who accompany Mary, the mother of Jesus.

One of the women is identified as Mary, the wife of Clopas. In Matthew and Mark, she is known as the mother of James and Joses. The James mentioned here is the disciple that we often call James the Less to distinguish him from James, the brother of John. We have no other information about this woman who sees our Lord suffer.[2]

The second woman we see identified in the shadow of the cross is Mary's sister. Mark tells us that her name is Salome and Matthew refers to her as the wife of Zebedee and the mother of James and John.[3] We should not find it surprising that John does not identify his mother by name since he rarely identifies himself in his Gospel. It seems his intention is to keep the attention entirely focused on Jesus.

We only see Salome at one other time in the Gospels.

✔ Read Matthew 20:20-28.

What request does this mother make of Jesus?

____

To what cup does Jesus refer?

____

How do the other disciples react to their request? Why?

____

● What valuable lesson does Jesus use this occasion to teach them?

____

____

As Jesus makes His final journey to Jerusalem, the mother of James and John comes to Jesus asking for positions of power and authority for her sons in His kingdom. Jesus alludes to the cup of suffering that He will soon drink and asks the two disciples if they can drink the cup He is about to drink. The men assure Jesus that they can and Jesus responds by telling them that they will drink from His cup. Indeed, these two men suffer much for the sake of the name of Christ. James is killed by Herod in Acts 12, and John is imprisoned for proclaiming the Gospel.

Jesus uses this opportunity to teach His followers that position and honor are not to be our goal. These the Father will bestow at His good pleasure. Rather, Jesus tells us that the way to true greatness in His kingdom is to serve. He uses His own life as an example.

Finish the words of Jesus' statement in Matthew 20:28.

"and to ____ "

 Jesus paid the ransom to free you from the bondage of the slavery of sin. The price required – His life. He considered you worth the ransom price.

The third woman we find standing in the shadow of the cross is Mary Magdalene. We are first introduced to Mary Magdalene in Luke 8:2.

What does Luke tell us about Mary Magdalene?

____

We know very little about this third Mary. Her name tells us that she is from the town of Magdala on the coast of the Sea of Galilee about three miles from Capernaum.[4] At one time in her life, she was afflicted with seven demons. Throughout the Gospels we see instances of Jesus casting evil spirits out of people, and while we are not given the specifics of her cure, we can be sure that the demons trembled at the name of Jesus. He not only proves Himself victorious over the physical world, He shows us that He has dominion over the spiritual world as well.

Despite not having a detailed biography of Mary Magdalene, we are given a powerful picture of the changed life of one who has been rescued by His mercy. In a sense, aren't we all like Mary Magdalene? We may not have been demon possessed, but each of us has been sin possessed, and only the love and grace of Jesus Christ is able to set us free.

There are two things about Mary's life of which we can be certain. First, she stands in the shadow of the cross because of her great love for Jesus. Unlike the disciples who have deserted Jesus, we see Mary at every step – from the cross, to the tomb, to the morning of His resurrection. She remains at her Savior's side, her heart bound to His out of great thankfulness and love. She knows clearly who has saved her, so she knows clearly whom she must follow.

● What can you learn from Mary Magdalene's love for Jesus?

____

____

● How do you see I John 4:19 displayed in Mary Magdalene's life? How is this truth displayed in your life?

____

____

____

● How do you make sure that your love for Jesus grows stronger every day?

____

____

The second characteristic of Mary Magdalene that deserves our consideration is how she uses her life after it was touched by the love and grace of Jesus.

✔ Read Matthew 27:55, Mark 15:41, and Luke 8:3.

To what kind of service does Mary Magdalene devote herself?

____

____

Mary Magdalene, along with other women, devotes her life and her fortune to meeting the needs of Jesus. These women provide the money that Jesus needs to carry on with His ministry throughout the countryside. Of course, they don't just send a check. They themselves travel with Jesus. They long to be close to Him, to daily learn His lessons, to meet whatever needs may arise, because He has met the deepest needs of their hearts.

● What needs of the Savior can you meet today?

____

____

1 Vines, p269
2 Edersheim, p602
3 Edersheim, p602
4 Lockyer, *All the Women of the Bible*, p100

Shadow Of Darkness

This week we stand solemnly on the hill of Golgotha as our Savior nears the climax of His work of salvation. As Jesus approaches death, we will listen as He cries out to His Father in pain and anguish of soul, voicing His humanity through the agony and proclaiming victory for all those who would come and stand in the shadow of the cross.

Day 1

✔ Read Matthew 27:45 and Luke 23:44-45a.

What unusual occurrence takes place at this time as Jesus hangs on the cross?

____

What time does this begin? How long does it last?

____

What do you think this means?

____

As the sixth hour approaches, we see a shift in the focus of the Gospels. For the first three hours that Jesus hangs on the cross, our attention is drawn to the people standing in the shadow of the cross – the soldiers, Jewish leaders, Mary and the other women, John, and the men condemned on either side of Him. Now we see the shadow of the cross engulfing Jesus. Our attention must now turn from those around the cross and focus solely on the Man on the cross.

From the sixth hour to the ninth hour (noon until three o'clock for our watches), we are told of a strange darkness covering the land. Luke gives us even more information, telling us that the sun stops shining. What an unusual sight for all of Israel! While it is unknown whether this darkness is global, the use of the word *land* indicates that this phenomenon is not just located at Golgotha but covers a wide area.[1] Even Roman historical accounts record this extraordinary event.

"Pilate sent the following report to Tiberius, emperor of Rome,

> And when he had been crucified, there was darkness over the whole earth, the sun having been completely hidden, and the heaven appearing dark, so that the stars appeared, but had at the same time their brightness darkened, as I suppose your reverence is not ignorant of, because in all the world they lighted lamps from the sixth hour until evening. And the moon, being like blood, did not shine the whole night, and yet she happened to be at the full."[2]

As the hour of Jesus' death draws nearer, the sky blackens into ebony. The blackness of our sin is reflected in the darkness of the sky. God darkens the sun to draw His people's attention to the face of His Son.

There are several ramifications that flow from this darkness over the land that deserve our attention.

First, this darkness that falls over the land helps to define a spiritual moment of new creation.

Look at Genesis 1:1-3.

At the beginning of creation, in what state was the world?

____

What is God's first act of creation?

____

In the beginning as God creates the physical world, He transforms the earth from a dark place to a place glistening with light. At the cross we see darkness again because God is creating a new world, spiritual in nature, that has a new light – the light of the Son.

Write Revelation 21:23.

____

____

When you become a Christian, a child of God, what transformation takes place within you?
Ephesians 5:8

____

● How is a child of light supposed to live? Ephesians 5:9-20

____

____

____

Second, we see the heart of our gracious God once again trying to reach the hard hearts of His stubborn people. Despite having centuries of preparation for the coming of the Messiah, many in Israel do not recognize Jesus when He is among them.

● Reading Isaiah 13:10, what light bulb do you think God wants to have go on in their minds and hearts when they see this darkness?

____

____

● How do we keep our hearts from becoming hard in the shadow of the great things that He has done for us?

____

____

____

Third, in what is perhaps its most important ramification, we once again see the price of our sin. As Jesus takes on our sin and pays the penalty for our unrighteousness, we see the withdrawal of the Father's presence.

What characterizes God's presence? I John 1:5 What do we see at this moment at the cross?

____

How do you see Amos 8:9-10 explaining God's actions at this moment?

____

____

God mourned for His only Son this day at Calvary. We, too, are called to mourn – not for the life of the Son, but for the necessity that brought about His death.

Define repentance.

____

In what way is mourning a part of repentance? 2 Corinthians 7:10

____

____

● Have you ever mourned your sin before the Lord? Describe your heart at that moment.

____

____

Write Matthew 5:4.

____

● What kind of comfort have you received from the Lord?

____

____

God comforts us with a comfort that cannot be duplicated by anything in the world. What joy, peace, and solace come from mourning our sins and breaking the stubborn places of our hearts before Him. Of course, God does not comfort us so that we might be comfortable, but rather that we should take His comfort with us and spread it on the wounded and broken hearts all around us.

Day 2

With the dark sky overhead, Jesus bears the full weight of sin's awful cost. Listen today as He cries out to His Father and only silence thunders in return.

✔ Read Matthew 27:46-47.

What time is it when Jesus cries out? How long has He been on the cross? (See Mark 15:25 for a reminder.)

____

What does Jesus say?

____

Look at your footnote. What Scripture does Jesus voice in His agony? Who else cried out these same words?

____

What misunderstanding occurs among those standing in the shadow of the cross?

____

The heart of Jesus cries out in loneliness and pain as He faces this most difficult moment. He has been on the cross for six hours now, and the moment of His death is imminent. The suffering for the sin of the world is almost complete. Added to the physical pain has been the overwhelming isolation that surrounds Him. This is His burden alone.

With a loud voice, He cries out, *"Eloi, Eloi, lama sabachthani?"* – which means, "My God, My God, why have you forsaken me?" The words of the psalmist David, in a combination of Aramaic and Hebrew, flow from Jesus' lips. The words of the ancestor of Christ speak powerfully of His utter desolation and the horror sin has wrought.

● Have you ever felt forsaken by God? Explain.

____

____

It is important to notice not only the words of Christ at this time, but the way in which they are spoken – with a loud voice. From a physical point of view, this is quite unusual. The longer a condemned man hangs on the cross, the weaker and more fragile his physical state becomes. With most men, crucifixion ends with unconsciousness leading to death. This will not be the case with Jesus. In order to defeat death, He must face death head on.

Those standing near the cross evidently misunderstand the first part of what Jesus says. They think that He is crying out to Elijah, the great prophet of the Old Testament. Of course, Jesus is crying out to One so much greater than Elijah. What truly dull hearts they have to believe that anyone other than God can save Him.

Of course, don't we do the same thing so many times? We look to and grab for anything or anyone who might have an answer for our crisis before we turn to the Word of God. The world can't save us. We can't even save ourselves. Only the mighty hand of God can rescue us.

● Have you ever gone to the world for answers before you went to God? What was the result?

____

____

Write Colossians 1:13-14.

____

✔ Read John 19:28-29 and Matthew 27:48-49.

What words does Jesus speak?

____

What is at least one of the reasons that Jesus voices His thirst at this time? Psalm 22:15

____

How does someone standing in the shadow of the cross respond to Jesus' cry?

____

How do the rest of the people near the cross react?

____

Jesus knows that the moment of death is approaching. He continues to submit His will in obedience to the Father and cries out that He thirsts. The excruciating pain and enormous blood loss that He has suffered over the last 16-18 hours has left His body crying out for fluids. His tremendous thirst just adds to the agony and torment of His torture.

His lips are parched and long for water just as His soul is parched without the refreshment of God.

● Has your soul ever felt dried and parched because you stayed away too long from the refreshment of God? Explain.

____

____

● Read Psalm 42:7-8. Describe the relief and joy that come when God quenches the aridity of your soul.

____

____

● How do we develop a thirst like that described in Psalm 42:1-2?

____

____

Just as daily our bodies need liquids, so daily our souls need the refreshment that can only be found in God's presence. There are days that I approach God so dry that my cup feels brittle. A strong breath of wind will blow the dust of my heart away. At these times He gently fills my need, refreshing me with quiet waters and calm streams. At other times I come into His presence overflowing with joy from the bounty of His goodness. His refreshment flows over me like a waterfall and I revel in His thundering glory.

When we are actively being the salt of the earth, it makes us thirsty for the Living Water!

Here we see the only act of mercy that is bestowed on Jesus during His agonizing ordeal. A man soaks a sponge in some wine vinegar, the cheap sour wine of the common people. He sticks the sponge on the end of a hyssop stalk that averages three to four feet in length. This he lifts to our Savior's lips. Impatient to see if His cry will bring a heavenly rescue, the rest of the crowd tells the man to leave Jesus alone as they watch curiously.

● Seeing the brief mercy that Jesus receives here, read Mark 9:41. What small mercies can you share with those in your life?

____

____

Day 3

Jesus is just moments away from death. The unbearable suffering reaches a peak and His physical body cannot stand the strain for much longer. While normally this moment would represent defeat and be filled with the dread of death, for Jesus this is a sweet moment of victory.

 Read John 19:30a.

What does Jesus say at this moment?

____

Brainstorm for just a minute. What is finished as Jesus dies on the cross?

____

____

John is the only Gospel writer that records this statement of Jesus, and I am so thankful that the Holy Spirit included it for us today. It is a profound statement about the work of Jesus on our behalf. Great comfort and many blessings flow from Jesus' words here, *"It is finished."*

We could have a grand theological discussion about the numerous things that are finished in the death and resurrection of Jesus – the sacrificial system, the priesthood, the Sabbath, the Mosiac Law, temple worship, the rules regarding food and external cleansing. Our list could go on and on. There are many books written about the completion and fulfillment of the Old Testament. The one I would recommend to you first is the book of Hebrews. The writer of Hebrews explores the concept of Christ's completion of the Old Covenant and all of its aspects in beautiful detail.

For our purposes, I would like to look at these words in a slightly different light. The words "It is finished" are not just meant to represent an end, but serve to open the door to a new beginning. With the fulfillment and completion of the old, Jesus offers His body as a new and living way to approach the Father.

Brainstorm again. What is beginning because Jesus died on the cross?

____

____

A New and Final Answer for Sin

✔ Read Romans 5:12-19.

Why does man need a final answer for sin?

____

____

● In what way do the actions of Adam represent us all?

____

Here Paul sets up a dramatic comparison between Adam and Christ that goes to the root of why we need a Savior.

In each of the columns below, note the progression that results from each one's actions.

	ADAM	JESUS	
Romans 5:19	_______________	_______________	Romans 5:19
Romans 5:19	_______________	_______________	Romans 5:15
Romans 5:12	_______________	_______________	Romans 5:16
Romans 5:16	_______________	_______________	Romans 5:17
Romans 5:16	_______________	_______________	Romans 5:17

When it is laid out in this way, our need for a plan of salvation is very clear. The actions of Adam in this passage outline the paths of each of our hearts. We are not under judgment because of Adam's sin, but rather Adam's disobedience opened the door for sin to enter the world. It is the same path that each of us have chosen. Our disobedience to the precepts of God are sinful before His holiness. The just result of sin is death, and in death there is judgment and condemnation. Eternal separation from God is our just punishment.

Jesus, from before the beginning of time, knew our need. He came to earth in the form of a man and, despite being in a world corrupted by sin, remained obedient and righteous. His obedience opened the door for God to offer us a marvelous gift – grace. When we accept this gift (and we must accept this gift in the manner that He chooses), we receive justification for our sins. We are clothed with His righteousness and receive life in His Name.

Read again Romans 5:17. How is God's grace described?

____

It is all we need. It is more than enough. And it is this gift of grace that He wraps in His own blood and offers to you from the shadow of the cross.

Sin has been man's burden since the Garden of Eden. Jesus picked up man's load of sin and carried it to the cross. When we come into contact with the blood of Jesus in the waters of baptism, the old person dies and a new person is born. This new person can joyously say, "It is finished!" – the old life, the sinful nature, the heavy weight of sin, the toll of guilt, it is all finished and done away with in the blood of Christ!

Write 2 Corinthians 5:17.

● In what ways have you said, "It is finished!" to the old you because of the blood of Jesus?

✔ Read Psalm 103:10-12.

Write the definition of grace that you see here.

● What kind of peace can you have knowing your sins have been "finished" in Christ?

Write Isaiah 1:18.

As white as snow. I can close my eyes and picture the landscape of my Minnesota childhood home in winter. All the seasons have their own beauty, but none brings a clearer picture of the new person I am in Christ than the recollection of newly fallen snow. There were many nights that I went to sleep having kicked my way through the dead leaves of fall, their brilliant color faded, lying on the ground as a testimony to the life and growing season now ended. In the light of morning, I would awake to a world transformed. Where yesterday there were the colors of death and decay, the world now glistens with the beauty of bright, white snow. The snow covering the ground is not just white. It is a blanket of brilliant, sparkling diamonds dancing in the sunlight. It is clean and fresh, pure and white. While the snow of my childhood never maintained this pristine beauty for long, the purity of our cleansing in Christ remains brilliant. As long as we remain in Christ, His blood provides a continual cleansing and our lives reflect the dazzling beauty of the Son.

Day 4

When Jesus spoke the words, "It is finished," He announced His completion of the purpose of God on our behalf and the opening of a whole new relationship between the Father and those who would become children of God through His blood. Today we will examine two more new beginnings given to us by Jesus in the shadow of the cross.

A New Family

In the Old Testament, God chose to have a special relationship with one physical nation – the children of Abraham. He set them apart and revealed Himself in many ways to them. They enjoyed the luxury of His blessings and His Presence lived among them between the cherubim above the mercy seat. He determined that it would be through the Israelites that the Savior would come.

Look at David's words in 2 Samuel 7:23-24. How does David describe Israel?

____

____

On the cross, how does Jesus finish this unique relationship with Israel and establish a new family relationship with all people?

____

____

When Jesus finished His work on the cross, He ended the special covenant relationship that was Israel's alone and opened an avenue for anyone to come to the Father by the power of His Name.

Read Revelation 5:9. To whom has salvation been offered? What price was paid to make this offer available?

____

____

The blood of Christ opens the doorway of grace to everyone – regardless of race, color, nationality, gender, or background. No longer would God's family be defined by their national origin but by the blood that transforms their hearts and the citizenship they are granted by becoming members of the kingdom.

What is the name of this new family? Ephesians 1:22

____

✔ Read Titus 2:11-14.

To whom has the grace of God appeared?

____

For what two things did Christ give Himself?

____

____

● What is your blessed hope? How does this hope define the way you live each day?

____

____

As we are transformed into the image of Christ by God's grace, what do we learn to do?

____

____

● How do these things make the family of God different from the world? In what way can the world tell that your life has been marked by the grace of God?

____

____

____

Christians are a new people, called to be pure in the midst of an impure world, eagerly awaiting the return of our Lord and Savior. As the family of God, we are called to honor the Father and work side by side with our brothers and sisters in Christ to invite the world into this new relationship in God. He has set us apart as a chosen people so *that you may declare the praises of him who called you out of darkness into his wonderful light.* I Peter 2:9b The beauty is that anyone may be a part of the God's household. We are set apart and separate from the world, not because only a few may be born a new creature in Christ, but because so few choose to be chosen.

What does God call you in Malachi 3:17?

____

On the cross, Jesus finished the work and opened the door that allows Him to present to the Father a brand new treasure – you.

A New Day of Victory Over Satan and Death

When Jesus declares on the cross "It is finished," He proclaims victory over the vile enemy set up in defiance to the throne of God and breaks his most painful weapon.

The battle has been raging for centuries. The heart of man the prize. Ever since Satan rebelled against the authority of God and was cast down from heaven, he has been trying to steal the heart of God's creation. Now the war has reached its critical climax. Although by every external indicator Jesus hangs defeated on a Roman cross, He is just moments away from ultimate victory. By submitting to death according to God's perfect plan, He will crush the death grip in which Satan has held the heart of man.

When Jesus cries in victory, "It is finished," He draws our attention again to the triumphant plan set in place before the creation of the world. Ephesians 1:4 God did not wait too long after creation to reveal His plan to us. Though its unfolding will take centuries, its revelation occurs at man's first moment of need.

Write Genesis 3:15.

____

____

____

Interestingly, to whom is this promise spoken? Why?

____

Who is the "he" to whom God refers? What will He do to the serpent? What will the serpent do to Him?

____

____

● In what way do you see God's eternal plan in these words?

____

Here, in the opening pages of the Bible, God reveals the *protoevangelium* – the first announcement of the Good News and in it we have our plan of salvation clearly laid out. One of the woman's offspring will one day rise up to crush the serpent. This is a specific reference to Jesus one day coming to earth in the form of a man. Now, think for a moment. How does one physically kill a snake? One would need to crush its head, perhaps with the heel of a shoe. As this crushing is taking place, the serpent raises its head and strikes the heel. The venom of the serpent will take its effect on the body, causing death. God tells us from the beginning that Jesus will die for our sins. But the picture does not end there. By His death and resurrection, the serpent will be completely crushed. Since Satan had presented himself in the physical form of a serpent to Eve, God presents him with a very physical picture of his ultimate defeat.

● How does knowing that Satan has been ultimately defeated change the way you look at world events?

____

____

● How does Jesus' victory over Satan help you live victoriously today?

____

____

● How do Jesus' words here change the way Christians approach and deal with death?

____

____

Jesus' victory changes everything. When our world is rocked by hatred, we can ground our hearts in the surety of His power and authority. When temptation nips at our heels, we can wrap ourselves in His presence. When death comes near and touches our hearts, we can bring our tears before Him and He will envelop us with His peace and the confidence that, for those that are His children, a different tomorrow will one day dawn.

Write I Corinthians 15:55-57.

____

____

____

"It is finished," Jesus cried as the moment of death neared. He finished paying the price for our salvation and provided a new and final plan to wash us clean. He finished the old covenant and established a new covenant with His blood. He sacrificed His own life to allow all men to come unto Him and be His chosen people. He defeated Satan and opened up a new avenue of victory in His Name. He finished the work of grace that we might be able to say with joy, "It is finished," and stand before Him scrubbed clean of sin by the blood of the Lamb. We need not be tormented by guilt or stooped under the weight of sin. We can run to Jesus and be washed completely clean and say to our sin and old way of life, "It is finished in Jesus."

---

1 Coffman, *Matthew*, p487
2 Coffman, *Matthew*, p488

Shadow Of Death

It is here. I can scarcely raise my eyes and look at the face of my Lord. As we stand in the shadow of the cross this week and watch the Son of God die for our sins, I pray that the hardness of our hearts will be shattered and a wellspring of praise and adoration will overflow into every area of our lives because of what He did for us in this moment.

Day 1

It is three o'clock in the afternoon. The sun that usually blazes overhead has been darkened as the Son of God is dying in the shadows below.

✔ Read Luke 23:46.

What does Jesus say as He dies? How does He say it?

____

____

What hope do you see in Jesus' words?

____

____

The moment of His death arrives. As the Son of God, He knows that His bodily functions are failing. What would seem like a moment of defeat and dread, Jesus infuses with hope and peace. He calls out to God with a loud voice, *"Father, into your hands I commit my spirit."*

Even in this final moment, we have much to learn from Jesus. *First,* as He cries out to His Father He reminds us of the intimate relationship He has with God. By calling out to His Father, He calls us again to a place of dependency and trust in the One who loves us so much.

● How do you build an intimate relationship with God? How are dependency and trust defining characteristics of such a relationship?

____

____

____

Secondly, in Jesus' words we see His calming reassurance that God is in control. He does not cry out for a rescue, nor does He berate those who falsely accuse Him. Instead He recognizes that this is the fulfillment of the Father's will. In times of crisis, our hearts need to remember that God is in control. There are times when the shadow of the evil one seems overwhelming in our lives. At other times, family, work, or health problems dominate our vision. At these moments we need to run back to the shadow of the cross and know that God will work out His purpose and will for His glory.

● Where in your life do you need to know that God is in control? Where in your life do you need to give God control?

____

____

____

Third, in Jesus' words we see one word that sums up what we as Christians need to do – commit.

● Explain below how and why each of these should be committed to God.

Your Heart ____

____

Your Soul ____

____

Your Mind

____

____

Your Strength (Body)

____

____

We need to strive daily to commit each aspect of our lives more fully to the Lord.

Commitment leads to overwhelming joy when He is the sole love of our hearts, the peace of our souls, the mindset of our intellect, and the strength of purpose and purity in our bodies. We must commit ourselves to Him in life so that we may confidently commit our souls to Him in death.

Finally, Jesus' words provide calm reassurance about the future of our souls. There are many today we hold to the view that there is no life beyond this life. Our society almost screams the motto that "this is it" and "you have to grab all the enjoyment you can." Nothing hurts my heart more than to go to a funeral of one who believed that this life is all that exists. No hope, only the darkness of death looms before them for eternity.

Jesus tells us this isn't true. He commits His spirit into the hands of His Father. There is nowhere in life or death that I would rather be. He holds the souls of His beloved children in the palm of His hand.

● Who do you know that needs this reassurance? How can you share that reassurance with them this week?

____

____

After committing His spirit into the hands of His Father, Jesus takes His last breath and dies. The hours of agony and pain have pushed His body into death.

Write I John 3:16a.

____

____

Doctors have studied the medical aspects of Jesus' death on the cross and offer us some insights as to the physical cause of His death. Many physical factors play a part in death by crucifixion – the dehydration and massive blood loss due to the brutal scourging that Jesus received was a large factor in the rapidity of His death. The fact that He could not carry the crossbeam shows us how weak He was before being nailed to the cross.

As we already discussed, the simple act of breathing is made excruciating on the cross. As Jesus fights for each breath, His body cannot completely dispel the carbon dioxide that gathers in the lungs. Over time, this carbon dioxide turns the blood acidic and results in a condition known as respiratory acidosis. As the acid builds in the bloodstream, it causes heart arrhythmias or an irregular heartbeat. Jesus would have felt the action of His heart becoming erratic and known that death was imminent. Doctors surmise that He died of cardiac arrest, otherwise known as a heart attack.[1]

With humble hearts we realize that He died of a heart attack so that He might destroy that which attacks our hearts.

Day 2

Jesus has died and God will not let His death pass without marking the moment with His power. Several remarkable things happen in the wake of Jesus' death and each leads us to the understanding that His might and His love have combined to provide a way for our salvation.

As we begin today, we need to take notice of one more important fact about the death of Jesus.

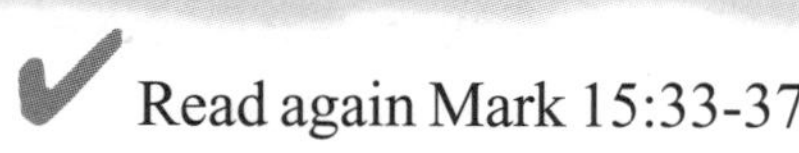Read again Mark 15:33-37.

What time does Jesus die?

____

For us, the timing of Jesus' death is fact and not much more, but for the Jews in Jerusalem for Passover, the time of His death takes on monumental importance.

 Read Exodus 12:21-27.

What is the purpose of Passover?

____

What is to be sacrificed by each Jewish family at Passover?

____

At the time of the Exodus, what did the blood of the lamb do for the Israelites?

____

Passover is a celebration of the mercy and deliverance of the Lord. As the tenth plague approached the land of Egypt, God commanded the Israelites to take an unblemished lamb, kill it, and use its blood to mark their doorways. When the destroyer was sent through Egypt, the blood of the lamb allowed death to pass over that home.

After centuries of celebrating the Passover, the Jewish rabbis and experts in the law had carefully regulated the time that the Passover lamb was to be sacrificed. At the time of Jesus, the lamb is to be sacrificed at three o'clock in the afternoon.[2] Jesus dies at the exact moment that the Passover lambs are being sacrificed!

How does 1 Corinthians 5:7 describe Jesus?

____

● How does His blood protect you from God's judgment of death?

____

____

At the moment of His death three miraculous things happen. These are meant to cement in the people's minds the moment when Jesus' work on the cross was finished and to testify to the power of God.

Read Matthew 27:50-53.

List the three things that occur at the moment Jesus dies.

____

____

____

We will spend today shaking with the tremors of the earthquake and standing in awe at open graves. Tomorrow we will go inside the temple and examine the veil.

● Why do you think that God would mark this moment with an earthquake?

____

____

How might Exodus 19:18 and Judges 5:5 help us understand this earthquake at Calvary?

____

____

As Moses and the people of Israel camped around Mount Sinai, God prepared to usher them into a covenant relationship with Himself. Here, on this mountain, He made them His own people and blessed them with His presence, provision, and protection. As the presence of God descended on the mountain, the earth trembled violently. This earthquake signaled the holiness of God and the importance of this occasion.

As we have already discussed, Jesus' death fulfills the old covenant and sets it aside. His blood provides the foundation for the new covenant by which we may come to the Father in obedience to Jesus' name. Just as an earthquake marked the initiation of the covenant established on Sinai, so God marks the establishment of this new covenant with an earthquake that highlights the holiness of God and the importance of this moment.[3]

In light of the earthquake here at the cross, write Isaiah 64:3.

____

____

____

Take a moment to thank God for the awesome and unexpected (from our perspective) things that He has done on your behalf.

● What significance do you see in the graves of the righteous being opened as Jesus dies on the cross?

____

____

It seems interesting that only the graves of holy people are opened. God indeed knows the hairs on our heads and the resting places of each of His people.

The graves being opened at Jesus' death gives us an almost prophetic picture of what will happen in just three days – the tomb will not be able to hold Jesus!

Not only do we have the opening of the graves, the holy people laid to rest in those tombs are raised to life! There is some difficulty in our understanding of the exact chronology of these events. When exactly these people were raised to life is unclear, but the language of the text seems to indicate that they did not come out of their tombs until after the resurrection of Jesus. At this time they made their way into the city of Jerusalem, providing proof and testimony of the resurrection power of God.[4]

● How does the physical resurrection of these holy people help us understand the spiritual resurrection that occurs in God's children?

____

____

Day 3

The third miracle that surrounds the death of Jesus holds powerful spiritual significance – the tearing of the curtain of the temple.

In order to understand the significance of God's actions at this moment, we need to familiarize ourselves with the blueprint of the temple and the purpose of the curtain.

 Read Exodus 25:8 and 26:30-35.

What is the purpose of the sanctuary?

____

Of what is the curtain to be made? What design is to be woven into the fabric?

____

____

In the space below, draw a diagram of the two rooms of the tabernacle. Label each, drawing a wavy line to show where the curtain hangs.

On your drawing above, show where the ark of the Testimony is located.

On Mount Sinai, God gave Moses detailed instructions for the construction of a tabernacle that would serve as His dwelling place among His people. It was to be completely transportable so that the children of Israel could take it with them on their journey from Egypt to the Promised Land. The tabernacle itself consisted of two rooms with a large courtyard. The larger of the two rooms is called the Holy Place and contained three pieces of furniture – the golden lamp stand, the table of the bread of the Presence, and the altar of incense. Each day the priests worked in this room trimming the lights, maintaining the incense, and weekly placing fresh bread on the table of the bread of the Presence.

Once a year the high priest was to enter the second room of the tabernacle – the Most Holy Place. He was to bring a sacrifice of blood to atone for the sins of himself and the people into the presence of God who dwelt between the cherubim on the ark of the Testimony. The elaborately woven curtain was called the shielding curtain (Numbers 4:5) and hid the ark from the eyes of the priests.

Approximately five hundred years later, King David desired to build God a more permanent dwelling. God did not allow David to do this but promised him that his son, Solomon, would build a house for His Name.

The temple at the time of Jesus is not the same one that Solomon built, but one rebuilt after a remnant of the kingdom of Judah returned from Babylonian captivity, and more recently renovated and expanded by Herod the Great. While much more elaborate and having many more rooms, at the center of the temple is the Holy Place and the Most Holy Place divided by a magnificent curtain.

According to tradition, the veil or curtain between the Holy Place and the Most Holy Place of the temple was 60 feet long and 30 feet wide. It was made up of 72 squares of fabric sewn together. Look at the palm of your hand. It is said that the thickness of the curtain could be measured by the width of a palm and that it was so heavy it took 300 priests to hold it up.[5]

What is unusual about the way the curtain was torn at Jesus' death?

____

Why do you think God did this?

____

____

✔ Read Hebrews 10:19-20.

By what means are we allowed to enter the Most Holy Place?

____

With what did Jesus replace the torn temple curtain?

____

God, in a very dramatic way, tears open the curtain that separates man and God. Up until this moment, only the high priest was allowed to enter God's presence and then only once a year. If he tried to go in at any other time, death would result. Now Jesus' own body is the curtain through which we must go in order to enter the presence of God. His blood opens a new and living way for all those who seek the Father's face and long to draw near to Him.

Write Ephesians 3:12.

____

● In what way does the blood of Jesus give you confidence to go into the presence of God?

____

____

Read Hebrews 10:22. What four things do we need in order to draw near to God?

____

____

____

We are allowed to draw near to God because of the confidence and access that is granted to us through the body and blood of Jesus.

Drawing near to God is a profound privilege. Because of the blood of Jesus we are able to have an intimate relationship with God. We are able to confidently go before Him because we come in the name of His Son.

What promise is made to us in James 4:8a?

____

● Is it possible to take too lightly our privilege of entering the Father's presence? Explain.

____

____

● Describe the other four "let us" actions outlined in Hebrews 10:19-25. How do each of these help us draw near to the presence of God?

____

____

____

Each time that we enter the presence of God, let us be overwhelmed with praise, and thanksgiving, and humility. God literally tore down the curtain that kept us from directly approaching His presence, and we are now allowed to see clearly the dazzling light of the Son.

Day 4

Today we go back to Calvary. Note the reactions of those who beheld these wondrous events and learn how we, too, should react in the shadow of the cross.

✔ Read Matthew 27:54.

Who do we see standing in the shadow of the cross at this moment?

____

What do they observe? What emotion do they experience?

____

Why do you think they were terrified?

____

● Have you ever been terrified before the Lord's awesome work? Explain.

____

____

What truth do they exclaim?

____

We go back and look now at the faces of the men whose job it is to carry out execution orders. Remember that each condemned man is assigned a squad of four soldiers and the entire contingent is under the command of a centurion, so there are at least thirteen soldiers in the shadow of the cross. You have to imagine that the hearts of these men whose job it is to crucify men week after week might be quite hardened to death and suffering. We have already seen them drinking, gambling, and throwing insults at Jesus earlier in the day. In this light, the reactions and words that flow from these coarse soldiers' tongues as Jesus dies on the cross are quite remarkable.

Darkness has been over the land for three hours. Then, as Jesus breathes His last, the earth begins to quake under their feet. Rocks are split apart, and tombs in the nearby garden break open. They had heard the words of the chief priests jeering at Jesus for being the Son of God. In this moment, the hardness falls away from their hearts and they stand terrified before God's power. They may be simple uneducated soldiers, but they can recognize the hand of God when they see it. They proclaim, *"Surely he was the Son of God."*

Why is it that the "educated" and "religious" Jews don't understand and the pagan Roman soldiers do? (Look back at the insults recorded in Matthew 27:43.)

____

____

● Is it possible for our "religious" knowledge to get in the way of seeing Jesus? Explain.

____

____

____

The centurion and the other soldiers at the cross declare with full certainty that Jesus is indeed the Son of God! There has been some question that the centurion does not declare that He is *the* Son of God but rather makes a pagan statement that Jesus is *a* son of God. However, the "Greek text does not at all necessitate the rendering 'a son'."[6] The Gospel writers clearly see this statement as a true declaration of the identity of Christ. He is indeed the Son of God!

Mark and Luke give us parallel accounts of the centurion's statement.

Read Mark 15:39 and Luke 23:47.

What additional information about the reaction of the centurion do Mark and Luke tell us?

____

____

Mark tells us that part of the centurion's confession was based on how Jesus died. After witnessing many crucifixions, it was very obvious that there was something different about our Lord. Seeing these differences made a profound impact on the heart of the centurion.

How is the way Jesus died similar to the way He lived?

____

____

● Has your walk with Jesus made such a dramatic impact in your life that the world can see the difference? Explain. Acts 4:13

____

____

Even in death, Jesus' behavior and attitude were different and attracted notice from the people who saw Him. If even in His death He reflected the love of God so profoundly, how much more should our lives be such that the world notices the difference!

Finally, Luke tells us the centurion praised God. What beautiful words! Imagine the transformation in the heart of this Roman soldier.

● Is praise the first thing that springs from your lips when you look at the Son of God? Explain.

____

____

The beautiful confession of the centurion is the foundation upon which all faith is built. It is the starting point of a relationship with God. If you believe that Jesus is the Son of God, then your heart can move forward and respond in obedience to His wonderful name.

✔ Read I John 4:15 and 5:10-12.

● How is acknowledging Jesus as the Son of God the first step in developing a relationship with God?

____

____

What testimony flows from this confession of faith?

____

____

What is the difference between one who believes that Jesus is the Son of God and one who does not?

____

____

John draws a very clear line – those who believe in the Son are on God's side; those who do not have nothing to do with God. In fact, they declare that God is a liar, because the testimony that God gave about His Son was false. Matthew 3:17 Those who believe and act in obedience to the truth that Jesus is the Son of God receive eternal life.

It is important to understand that this confession of faith is two-fold. When we first come to Christ, we are called to publicly confess our belief that Jesus is the Son of God. This confession spurs us to obedience, and we are buried with Him in baptism and become children of God. Romans 10:9-10, I Timothy 6:12, and Mark 16:16 are our example.

Our confession, however, does not end there. Our lives, from the moment we arise a new creature from the waters of baptism, should be a continual confession of the Son of God who so powerfully saves us. The way you act, talk, treat others, spend your money, raise your children, dress, entertain yourself, and the myriad of other things we do give a daily confession about our belief that Jesus is the Son of God.

Write Hebrews 13:15. Circle how often we are to praise and confess His Name.

____

____

What will result from a life lived confessing that Jesus is the Son of God? 2 Corinthians 9:13

____

There is one more group that stands in the shadow of the cross – a group of witnesses, evidently not close friends of the Savior but observers of the events at Golgotha, that merit our attention.

✔ Read Luke 23:48-49.

How do these witnesses react to the events at the cross?

____

In our culture this action has very little meaning, but to the reader of the day, it was understood to be a sign of anguish and repentance. Whatever these observers knew about Jesus before His death, the events at the cross brought the recognition that God's hand had been with Him.

● Look at Jeremiah 31:19 and Luke 18:13. How do you express your humility and unworthiness before God?

____

____

1 Strobel, p199
2 Clarke, p849
3 Coffman, *Matthew*, p493
4 Coffman, *Matthew*, p494
5 Edersheim, p611
6 Coffman, *Mark*, p307

Shadow Of The Grave

This week we will see the death of Jesus proven beyond a shadow of a doubt and His burial in the tomb of a rich disciple. It is a time of great sorrow for those that love Jesus, and it is easy for us to overlook their grief because we know the rest of the story. Praise God that we do! This week feel the grief and the sorrow that flow from those who loved Him even in death. Only in understanding their grief can we appreciate their joy.

Day 1

✔ Read John 19:31-37.

What request do the Jews make of Pilate? Why? Does Pilate grant their request?

____

____

What do the soldiers do to the two men crucified on either side of Jesus? What does this tell you about their condition?

____

Why do they not break the legs of Jesus?

____

What does the soldier do instead? Why?

____

____

What unusual sight do those around the cross observe? John 19:34

____

● Why do you think this makes such a profound impression on John?

____

____

What is the significance of the fulfillment of prophecy by the soldiers?

____

____

It is the Preparation Day before the special Sabbath that marks Passover. As the afternoon nears its end and the sunset announces the beginning of the Sabbath, the Jews do not want the bodies of the criminals left on the crosses. This would be a violation of the Law.

Read Deuteronomy 21:22-23. What instructions does the Law give regarding the timing of execution and burial?

____

What pronouncement does God make about those condemned?

____

How does Galatians 3:13 describe Jesus?

____

Jesus carried the weight of God's curse so that we could experience the delight of His blessings.

Again we see the hard hearts of the Jewish leaders. They are concerned about not defiling the Sabbath and fail to see that they have killed the Lord of the Sabbath. (Matthew 12:8) May we never get so caught up in religion that we lose sight of Jesus.

The Jews go to Pilate and ask for the *crurifragium* to be carried out. This involves using some sort of large hammer or beam to break the legs of the crucified.[1] With their legs broken, the dying men are unable to push upward to take a breath and death by asphyxiation rapidly takes place. Pilate grants the Jewish request and orders the soldiers to break the legs of the prisoners.

The soldiers approach one of the men on Jesus' side and break his legs. Then they rapidly move to Jesus' other side and do the same thing. This tells us that these two men are still visibly alive. As the soldiers approach Jesus, they take note that He is already dead and do not break His legs. Instead, a soldier draws his spear and plunges it into the Savior's side. It seems that His intent is to prove that Jesus is truly dead.

● Why is this action by a Roman of great importance to the Gospel story?

____

____

As the soldier withdraws his spear from Jesus' side, blood and water flow out of the wound. This unusual mixture appears to be the result of the erratic, rapid heartbeat that Jesus experienced before death. As His heart raced to pump the low volume of blood that remained in His body, fluid collected in the sac that surrounds the heart, called the pericardium. This is a medical condition called pericardial effusion. In addition, fluid probably collected in the lungs as well which is known medically as pleural effusion. When the soldier thrusts the spear in Jesus' side (traditionally the right side which is supported by the medical information), he pierces the lung and the heart. As he withdraws the spear, a rush of this clear effusion liquid gushes forth, as well as blood that had pooled in the heart after death.[2] Of course, the blood would appear more shocking, especially to the loving eyes of John, which is perhaps why he mentions it first.

This action, and the flow of blood and water, makes such a profound impression on John that he emphasizes the truth of his testimony. It seems that John, once again, is speaking of himself in the third person, which is his custom throughout his Gospel.

● You are the jury and John is the eyewitness testifying to what he has seen in the shadow of the cross. What is your verdict?

____

____

The blood and the water that flow from Jesus' side are important for us to examine. The *first and most important* observation that comes from this account is the absolute certainty that Jesus is dead. There are those today who claim that Jesus did not really die on the cross but just fainted. The record we have here in John destroys this accusation. To deny that Jesus died on the cross is to deny the foundation of our hope. The independent actions of the Roman soldier lay waste to the claim that Jesus' death was all a hoax.

Second, we see over and over again the certainty that God is in control of every aspect of Jesus' death. The Roman governor has given orders that the legs of the criminals be broken. However, when the soldier sees that Jesus is dead he decides not to break His legs. Instead, the soldier acts independently of the governor's instructions and thrusts his spear in Jesus' side.

God controlled that moment just as He holds all our moments in His hand. Through the prophets, God had foretold that not a bone would be broken in Christ's body and that He would be pierced. This is exactly what happens despite the fact that an unusual set of behavior had to occur for it to happen.

● Why is it important that we see God's presence in every moment when we stand in the shadow of the cross?

____

____

Day 2

Now that Jesus has been proven dead by the Roman spear, our attention turns to His burial. Out of the shadow of fear, we see two prominent men come forward to honor the body of Jesus.

✔ Read Matthew 27:57-60, Mark 15:42-45, Luke 23:50-52, and John 19:38.

Using all four Gospel accounts, make a list of all that we are told about the man named Joseph.

____

____

____

What request does Joseph make of Pilate?

____

How is this request described? How does this request differ from his earlier behavior?

____

What is Pilate's reaction to this request?

____

What information does he verify? Why is this important?

____

Even though this is our first glimpse of Joseph of Arimathea, we are given a great deal of information about him. Joseph is from the Judean town of Arimathea located about 20 miles northwest of Jerusalem.[3] He is a wealthy man and a prominent member of the Sanhedrin, the Jewish ruling council. This tells us that he is well educated and a member of the Jewish elite. Despite being a member of the council that put Jesus to death, Luke makes it very clear that he was not a party to these actions. Since Mark 14:64 states that all that were present condemned Jesus to death, it is reasonable to think that Joseph and Nicodemus, whom we will meet later, were not present at these meetings.

We are also given a sketch of Joseph's character. He is a good and upright man. What a wonderful legacy! We should all desire to be known as good and upright by all we meet.

Joseph of Arimathea is also a man who is waiting for the kingdom of God. Perhaps this is what led him to listen to the teachings of Jesus and then to become a disciple. Over and over Jesus proclaimed the coming of the kingdom of God!

Look at Luke 4:43 and 17:20-21 and note what Jesus said about the kingdom of God.

____

____

The only negative note that is mentioned at all about Joseph is that he is a disciple in secret because he fears the Jews.

● What in his life does Joseph fear will be compromised if it is discovered that he is a disciple of Jesus?

____

____

What moment inevitably comes for anyone afraid to confess the name of Jesus? How does Joseph handle this moment?

____

____

● Are there ever moments when you choose not to talk about Jesus in order to fit in? Explain.

____

____

Being a disciple of Christ has many blessings but also demands a heart and soul commitment. God does not allow us to be "half-way" Christians. We must fully embrace Him and allow His love to transform every area of our lives.

Joseph is a man who eagerly anticipates the kingdom of God. In Jesus, He finds the fulfillment of his hope. Yet, he does not fully embrace discipleship. He is afraid of the Jews, and this can only mean that he fears for his position and wealth. If the other members of the Sanhedrin learn of his acceptance of Jesus' teaching, he can be forced out with great personal embarrassment.

At the moment of Jesus' death, we see the heart of Joseph of Arimathea change. He goes boldly to Pilate and asks for the body of Jesus. Remember what he is putting on the line with this request — word is sure to get back to the Sanhedrin of his actions on Jesus' behalf. Here we see love for Jesus melting fear, and Joseph acts to honor the body of the One he followed from afar.

● Where in your life do you need to imitate Joseph and boldly proclaim your love for Jesus?

____

____

Mark is the only one who records for us Pilate's reaction to Joseph's request. He is stunned that Jesus is already dead. While we have stretched the events out so we can look at each one, we need to remember that some of these things overlap and happen very rapidly. It has probably been only a very short while since Pilate gave the order to break the prisoners' legs, and now a man appears requesting Jesus' body for burial.

Normally, it is the Roman custom to allow the bodies of the crucified to hang on the cross until all the flesh is torn away by birds or animals. Caesar Augustus, however, granted special favor to the Jews and allowed them to remove the bodies from the crosses and bury them before the onset of the Sabbath, after it has been proven that they are truly dead.[4]

As sunset and the onset of the special Passover Sabbath quickly approaches, Joseph is in a hurry to claim the body of Jesus. Pilate summons the centurion from Golgotha and inquires if Jesus is really dead. The centurion assures Pilate that He is dead, and Pilate grants the release of Jesus' body to Joseph.

Again we see God laying the careful foundation for what will happen on Sunday. He layers the proof of Jesus' death with the testimony of multiple witnesses so that the power of God will have a mighty showcase in just three days. Here even the Roman government itself gives testimony to the fact that Jesus is dead.

● What benefit is there for you that God has so carefully documented each moment of Jesus' death?

____

____

Day 3

Jesus is dead and the authority of the Roman government itself confirms the truth of His death. Now as the sun crawls toward the horizon in the west, two men who followed Jesus from afar tenderly bury the body of Israel's Messiah.

 Read John 19:39.

Who joins Joseph in receiving Jesus' body?

____

Look back at John 3:1-21. What do we know about this man?

____

____

____

What supplies does Nicodemus bring with him?

____

Very early in Jesus' ministry, John tells us about another secret believer who comes by night to question Jesus. His name is Nicodemus. He is a Pharisee and another member of the Sanhedrin. This information tells us that, much like Joseph of Arimathea, Nicodemus is wealthy and well educated.

What information about the kingdom of God does Jesus give Nicodemus? John 3:3

____

After this visit with Jesus, Nicodemus fades into the night and we are unsure whether he heeds the words of Jesus. At the time of Jesus' death however, he, like Joseph, declares his allegiance.

Now as the sun sets in the west, two men whose faith had been hidden during His life, openly commit themselves to honoring Jesus in His death.

● What can you do today to show honor to Jesus?

____

____

Nicodemus comes prepared to bury Jesus properly. He has gathered fragrant spices, a mixture of myrrh and aloes, with which to wrap the body. This expensive blend of spices will be his final offering to Jesus.

Read John 19:41-42. Describe the location of the tomb in which Jesus will be laid.

____

Read Matthew 27:60. Who owns the tomb? Describe the tomb.

____

____

Time is now the enemy of Joseph and Nicodemus. The special Sabbath honoring the Passover is rapidly approaching. It is necessary to quickly move the body of Jesus from the execution site to the place of burial. Near Golgotha is a garden in which Joseph has hewn for himself and his family a tomb out of the rock. It is here that they will bury Jesus.

Based on similar tombs constructed during this time we can get a rough idea of what the tomb is like. It was cave-like in appearance, approximately six feet in width and height and nine feet in length. Into the wall one would find carved niches into which the bodies are placed. A large disk-shaped stone is rolled onto a grooved track to seal the entrance and held into place by a smaller stone.[5] The entrance stone is so massive in size and weight that one person cannot move it.

Another piece of information we are given is that this is a new tomb that had never been used. Again what seems like just interesting information is proof of God's power that will be displayed at the resurrection.

Read 2 Kings 13:21. What happened at this burial?

____

In this light, why does God tell us that the tomb of Jesus is new and unused?

____

____

God carefully builds the foundation on which our faith will rest. In many ways, He eliminates and neutralizes objections and accusations that will arise in an attempt to deny the resurrection. Here God assures us that Jesus' resurrection will be based on God's power alone and not some contact with a prophet's old bones.[6]

✔ Read John 19:40.

Describe how the body of Jesus is prepared for burial.

____

____

Taking a large piece of linen cloth and the spices brought by Nicodemus, the men begin the burial process. Tearing the cloth into strips that look like long rolled bandages, they carefully wrap Jesus' body, pressing in the spices between the layers of fabric. While they are pressed for time, we can only imagine that this is done with great dignity and love. They then place a cloth around Jesus' head and position Him in the tomb. Feel the heaviness of their hearts as they struggle to move the huge stone in front of the entrance to the tomb. As the heavy stone falls into place, they cannot imagine that this most somber and sorrowful place will soon reveal itself to be a place of victory for the entire world.

Day 4

I approach this lesson with great hope and anticipation. Soon we will get to talk about the resurrection. Nothing is more thrilling! However, we must remember at this moment, approximately two thousand years ago, grief and sorrow defined the moment, not anticipation. As the sun heads into the west, many of Jesus' closest disciples feel that the light of Israel has been extinguished.

✔ Read Matthew 27:61 and Luke 23:55-56.

Who else witnesses the burial of Jesus? Of what do they take note?

____

What do they prepare for Jesus' body?

____

Mary Magdalene and Mary, the mother of James and Joses, watch the two men prepare the body for burial. They take careful note of where the tomb of Jesus is located and how the body is laid within it. They have it in their hearts to also honor Jesus. In their grief they return home and prepare spices and perfume to place on the body, but with the Sabbath rapidly approaching, they must sit quietly with grieving hearts and obey God's command to do no work.

Read Matthew 27:62-66.

What new worry is now plaguing the Pharisees?

____

What request do they make of Pilate? What do they fear will happen? How do they secure the tomb?

____

____

One would think that the Pharisees and the rest of the Jewish leadership would be home celebrating their resolution of the problem of Jesus. Instead, we find them recalling His words.

What sign did Jesus promise the Pharisees? Matthew 12:38-40

____

____

What had Jesus explained to His disciples? Matthew 16:21-22

____

____

● Why do you think we see the enemies of Jesus recalling His words now when His disciples do not seem to remember them?

____

____

● Do you ever find it difficult to focus on the promises of Jesus when you are surrounded by crisis and turmoil? How do we learn to depend on Him even when things seem their darkest?

____

____

____

Just when they think they have solved all of their troubles, they remember Jesus' words. They will see the sign of Jonah – the heart of the earth will hold the Son of Man for three days and three nights. Remember one of the great downfalls of these leaders is their love of their positions among the people. All they need is for the disciples of Jesus to steal the body and then claim that He has arisen from the dead. Then they might never be able to stomp out His popularity and following.

The Pharisees once again approach Pilate. He has granted almost every request, and now they beg him to grant one more. They ask the Governor to secure the tomb until the third day so that it will be impossible for the disciples to disturb the body.

Pilate, who doesn't desire another religious uproar from the contentious Jews, grants their request. He gives them a Roman guard and allows them to secure the tomb. The Jews station the soldiers to guard the tomb and further secure the grave by putting a seal on the stone. This way, if the rock covering the opening to the tomb is disturbed in any way, the seal will be broken and they will know that someone entered the tomb.

Evening has fallen and our hearts are as dark with sorrow as the sky is black with night. Jesus is dead. His tortured body has been lovingly wrapped and laid in a nearby grave. Guards and seals have been put in place to hold Him within the tomb's walls.

Recalling all you have learned about Jesus' death, read Romans 5:6-8, writing verse 8 on the lines below.

____

____

Once again let humility, praise, and gratitude flow from your heart. Write a note of praise and adoration to your Savior.

____

____

____

As we sit in the garden in front of the tomb that holds our Lord's body, we can't help but notice the parallel. Man's fall into sin, which forced him out of the presence of God, happened in a garden. Soon, in another garden, the opportunity to once again enter the presence of God will be proclaimed by the echoes of an empty tomb. But for now we wait…for three days.

---

1 Edersheim, p613
2 Strobel, p199
3 *NIV Study Bible*, p1488
4 Bishop, p510
5 Edersheim, p318
6 Coffman, *Luke*, p456

Shadow Of Victory

This week we finish our journey that began in the shadows of the garden of Gethsemane. The journey that leads to the shadow of the cross is sobering, humbling, and exciting. It is here at the cross and the nearby tomb that the foundation of our joy and hope are born. Jesus died on the cross to pay the price for our sins. He rose on the third day to give us the glorious hope of a new life. This is a journey that we should make often. We must daily root our hearts in the love we see displayed in the shadow of the cross and allow our souls to depend on the power proclaimed by the empty tomb.

Day 1

I am so excited that I can barely type these words. This week we see the power of God displayed in all its glory as Jesus emerges from the tomb, victorious over death. As you begin this lesson, I pray that your heart will tremble with anticipation and jump for joy as we watch the events of this Sunday morning unfold. Ask God to fill your heart with awe as you see His mighty hand. Stop often and praise His glorious Name!

The events that unfold on Sunday morning are recorded by all four Gospel writers. The chronology is somewhat difficult to pin down as there are different groups of people moving in and out of the garden, running to and from the tomb, and spreading the news to others. Each of the Gospel writers records different details, and we will do our best to work through a fair timeline of these amazing events. Through all the different reports one supreme truth comes shining through – the tomb is empty and Jesus is alive!

✔ Read Matthew 28:2-4.

How does God announce the resurrection?

____

Who rolls away the stone? Describe him.

____

____

What is the reaction of the soldiers?

____

Just as God focused attention on Jesus' death with an earthquake, so the moment of His resurrection is announced with the earth violently trembling. An angel of the Lord descends from heaven, brilliant in appearance, and rolls back the heavy stone from the entrance to the tomb. It seems that he is sent, not to help Jesus come out of the tomb as God's power is more than sufficient for that, but rather to prepare the grave for the eyewitnesses who will testify that the tomb is empty! The events that occur at dawn so frighten the guards that they become like dead men.

✔ Read Matthew 28:1, Mark 16:1-4, and Luke 24:1-10.

Who do we see heading for the tomb?

____

What are they going to do?

____

What problem do they discuss?

____

What do they find upon reaching the tomb?

____

____

As the night sky turns to gray and the sun begins its climb in the east, some women who love Jesus begin making their way to His tomb. They carry in their arms spices which they are going to work into the wrapping covering Jesus' body. They want to offer this one last gesture of honor and love to the One who had treated them with honor and love. Little do they know what awaits them!

The Gospel writers name four women and Luke tells us that there are *"others with them"* as well. On the way they discuss the practical – who will move the heavy stone blocking the entrance? Imagine their surprise as they approach the place where Jesus is buried and see the stone already rolled away. As they near the tomb, they look inside and the tomb is empty!

It seems best to understand at this time that Mary Magdalene, stunned by the disappearance of Jesus' body, leaves the group of women and goes to find Peter and John.

Read John 20:1-2. What does she tell the disciples?

____

____

While the women stand amazed at the empty tomb, the guards are conferring with members of the Sanhedrin.

Read Matthew 28:11-15.

When do some of the guards leave the tomb?

____

What report do they give the chief priests?

____

What lie do the chief priests invent to cover up the truth of the resurrection?

____

What offer to they make to the guards?

____

● Why do you think the chief priests don't just believe at this moment?

____

____

At the same time that the women are approaching the tomb, the frightened guards leave after witnessing the miraculous events that occur. They report to the chief priests and pour out their story of the violent earthquake, an angel of dazzling light rolling away the stone, and their own reaction to these momentous events. One can only imagine the look of stunned disbelief that registers on the faces of the chief priests as the guards' story unfolds.

The chief priests quickly gather the elders together and devise a plan to try to counteract the amazing truth of Jesus' resurrection. It seems unimaginable to me to think that they don't even give a moment's pause to consider that Jesus might actually be who He says He is.

The plan the chief priests and elders devise springs from the original excuse they gave Pilate in requesting guards at the tomb – the disciples have stolen His body while the guards slept. They convince the guards to circulate the story by offering them money to tell the lie. Of course, falling asleep on the job might get them in trouble, but the leaders promise to intercede on their behalves with the governor. The guards agree to the deception and the lie is spread among the Jews.

● Are there people today with such hard hearts that no matter how the resurrection is presented to them they refuse to believe in it? How do we keep our hearts tender to the resurrection story?

____

____

____

How might Matthew 28:11-15 combined with Matthew 27:51 explain Acts 6:7?

____

____

Day 2

The tomb is empty! Jesus is alive! Is your heart pounding? This is the most amazing moment you will ever encounter. In this moment God extends the power of transformation and reconciliation to you. It is because of the power He reveals here that we have hope and joy. Today we will listen as God begins to spread the news about the resurrection. Soon the news will be a tidal wave, powerful and unstoppable, bringing refreshment and salvation to the whole world.

✔ Read Matthew 28:5-7, Mark 16:5-8, and Luke 24:4-8.

Whom do the women see upon entering the tomb? Describe their appearance.

____

____

What is the reaction of the women to this sight?

____

What amazing question does the angel ask the women?

____

What glorious news does the angel proclaim?

____

Of what teaching of Jesus does the angel remind the women?

____

____

What instructions does the angel give to the women?

____

____

As they enter the empty tomb two angels – lightening bright in appearance, greet the women. The fact that Matthew and Mark record the words of one angel gives us confidence, because we see the truth of varying eyewitness accounts. It may also be that Matthew and Mark focus on the angel who speaks because his words announce the most important event of all time.

Angels joyfully announced His birth from the womb. As Jesus now emerges from the tomb, we once again see angels proclaiming the good tidings with great joy!

Frightened by the appearance of the heavenly messenger, the women bow their faces to the ground. Here we hear the joyous news ring out, *"Why do you look for the living among the dead? He is not here; he is risen!"* Luke 24:5b-6a

● What victory do we find in the words of the angel?

____

____

The joyous words of the angel are not only for the women physically standing in the empty tomb. They ring out for all who come to gaze through its open door.

The angel then shows them the place where His body had lain as proof that He has risen. He reminds them of Jesus' own words about the suffering He would endure, His death, and the fact that He would rise again in three days. Jesus prepared them for this moment, but they had not anticipated the reality of what He had told them. Of course, the spiritual ramifications of the resurrection will not be fully revealed until Pentecost. The angel gives the women an important instruction – they are to go and tell the disciples the good news that Jesus has risen.

● In what way are we given the same instruction? How are you carrying out this instruction?

____

____

____

Mark records the immediate reaction of the women. They are trembling and bewildered. Imagine how hard it would be to absorb the news they have just heard. The women have spent the last three days in mourning and grief. They come to the tomb to pay respect to the body of the Lord and instead they are told He is alive! These devoted followers of Christ are stunned and frightened by this overwhelming news and flee the tomb.

Write Matthew 28:8.

____

____

Once they have had a few moments to process the amazing news, they are filled with joy and rush to tell the disciples.

● Does the resurrection fill your heart with joy? How do we keep the resurrection the central focus of our hearts?

____

____

As the women hurry off to tell the disciples, we find that Mary Magdalene has already taken the news of the empty tomb to Peter and John.

✔ Read John 20:3-9 and Luke 24:12.

How do these two disciples get to the tomb? Who gets there first?

____

Who goes into the tomb first? What do they see?

____

____

What is John's reaction to the empty tomb?

____

What is Peter's reaction to the empty tomb?

____

● Why do you think that the women are met with angels proclaiming the good news and Peter and John are met by silence?

____

____

Mary seems to have missed the announcement of the angel in the tomb. She runs to Peter and John and tells them that the body of Jesus is missing. I just love the fact that they run to the tomb. How our hearts should race as well when we contemplate the empty tomb! John, being somewhat younger and faster, reaches the tomb first.[1] He looks in and sees the strips of cloth lying in the tomb but dares not enter. Peter catches up and, just as you would expect, goes right in. They stand in wonder as they look at the strips of linen cloth lying where His body had been. The burial cloth that had been wrapped around His head is lying off by itself, neatly folded.

The reactions of the two disciples are recorded for us. John sees the empty tomb and believes. While he does not understand all of the spiritual theology and ramifications of Jesus' resurrection, John saw Him die and now he knows that Jesus is alive.

Peter leaves the tomb pondering the mystery of God that is unfolding. We must assume that the last three days have been extremely hard on Peter. Having denied the Lord three times and knowing the Jesus was aware of his failure, he never has a chance to seek Jesus' forgiveness before His death. The heart-wrenching grief has been compounded by guilt, remorse, and self-recrimination. His wounded heart needs time to absorb the earth-shattering news of Jesus' resurrection.

● What are some different ways that people react to the news of the resurrection today? What is your reaction to the resurrection?

____

____

An interesting note before John and Peter leave the garden tomb. Earlier when the group of women approached the open grave and, in tomorrow's lesson, when we rejoin Mary Magdalene at the tomb, we see angels there proclaiming the news of the risen Savior. Yet, when Peter and John go in, the tomb is completely empty. We might wonder why the men did not receive the glorious news by these messengers from heaven in the same way the women did. While we cannot understand all of God's wisdom in the way He chooses to deal with man, I think that, at least in part, the answer is simple.

Peter and John will spend the rest of their lives testifying about what they did not see in the tomb that Sunday morning. I believe that for these men whose responsibility it would be to spread the resurrection story throughout the world, God wanted no distractions to take their attention away from the fact that Jesus was not in that tomb. It was completely empty. Totally silent. The truth of their testimony will be severely tested over their lifetimes. They will be imprisoned and persecuted for proclaiming that Jesus is alive and the tomb is empty. God wants the image of complete emptiness seared on their minds and hearts. He wants their total focus to be on Jesus.

That is where God wants your focus to be as well – totally centered on Jesus. The world will parade a dazzling display of distractions to lure your attention away from your risen Savior. In those moments, go once again to the empty tomb. Here your voice echo off the walls. Focus your heart again completely on Jesus and rejoice that He lives!!

Day 3

The long night of grief has dawned bringing inexpressible joy. Hearts bowed with sorrow are given wings of hope. It is this same joy and hope that the Savior extends to your bruised heart as well. Our souls can soar before His throne because He lives. Today we will witness a most amazing, yet gentle and heart-touching moment. The risen Savior approaches one who loves Him wholeheartedly.

✔ Read John 20:10-18.

Briefly recall what you know about Mary Magdalene.

____

____

Why is Mary weeping?

____

Who does she see in the tomb? How does her reaction differ from the other women?

____

____

What does Mary Magdalene not yet realize? How do you think her sorrow interferes with her ability to recognize the truth?

____

____

Who does she then see? Why doesn't she recognize Him?

____

____

What does she ask Him?

____

How does He respond to her? What does she do when she recognizes Jesus?

____

____

As soon as Mary tells Peter and John about the empty tomb, they run for the garden. They rush off leaving Mary on her own to catch up with them. Upon arriving back at the tomb Mary is confused and overwhelmed with grief. She stays at the tomb crying. Realize that these are no gentle tears running silently down her cheeks. The Greek word used here indicates that Mary is sobbing and wailing aloud in her grief.[2]

As she bends over to look in the tomb, she sees two angels, dressed in white, sitting where His head and feet once rested. They ask her why she is crying. Death has been conquered and Jesus is alive! Only Mary does not yet have this fantastic news.

Here, in Mary Magdalene, we have a picture of ourselves. Before we come to know Jesus and the power of His resurrection, we are bowed with pain and tears. All hope is dead. Sorrow and desolation are our only companions. Watch for the transforming power that comes from standing before the risen Jesus.

Despite the heavenly scene before her, Mary does not seem to react to the presence of the angels. Her only thought is of Jesus. O, how I wish we could imitate her — to have the whole of our hearts and minds focused only on our Lord. Her overwhelming love and single-minded focus are most beautiful.

Unlike with the other women, the angels do not tell Mary the good news. Jesus is watching her tears and will tell her personally of His resurrection. Mary turns around and, as her eyes and heart are so overwhelmed with tears and grief, she does not recognize Jesus to be the One standing before her. She believes Him to be the gardener and begs once again for the body of her Lord.

Jesus speaks one word – her name. I imagine the voice of Jesus to be so gentle, so full of love. Mary turns toward Him, her heart exploding with wonder, amazement, and joy. She cries out, *"Rabboni!"* which means Teacher. From Jesus' words in John 20:17, we also get the picture that Mary tightly holds on to Him, perhaps afraid that she will never see Him again.

● How does it feel to know that Jesus knows your name? John 10:3.

____

____

● Why do you think that Jesus shows Himself to Mary Magdalene first?

____

____

● How do the next words that Jesus speaks to Mary in John 20:17 reveal the new door that Jesus has opened by His blood?

____

____

Jesus knows your name. He knows how to pronounce it, and it is spelled correctly in the Book of Life! Knowing someone's name is a sign of friendship and intimacy. Despite being Lord of all the earth, He knows you individually and loves you with a singular passion.

Here the work of salvation is revealed. No longer are the eleven just disciples, Jesus calls them "*my brothers*." The relationship that He shares with the Father is available to all. With the opening of the tomb, Jesus opens the door for all who come in His Name to enter into the presence of God.

✔ Read John 20:18 and Mark 16:9-11.

How do others react to Mary's joyous news?

____

Jesus' second appearance is to the group of women we saw previously at the tomb.

✔ Read Matthew 28:9-10.

How does Jesus appear to them? What does He say?

____

What do the women do after Jesus greets them?

____

● In what way should this be our reaction every time we come before Him?

____

____

Jesus bestows on the women a great mercy. Mary Magdalene and this group of women are the first to see Him alive. He could have shown Himself to Peter and John when they came to the tomb, but He chose to bring joy to the women first. Remember, all of the disciples, save John, have deserted Him, but the women have not. In the shadow of the cross, we see the women staying by Jesus' side.

Even after His death, they follow Joseph and Nicodemus to the tomb so they know where He is laid. They return as early as the Law allows to honor His body. Jesus honors their love by making His presence known to them first. He is first in their hearts and Jesus allows them the grace of seeing Him first.

● How will it change your life to honor Him first in your heart?

____

____

Day 4

We could do another study on the appearances of Jesus after His resurrection. The ones we have looked at occur during the first hour on that Sunday morning. We know that He is reunited with Peter, freely giving forgiveness to Peter's repentant heart. He meets with the disciples multiple times and even quiets the doubting of Thomas' heart. He walks the road to Emmaus and appears to more than five hundred at one time. (1 Corinthians 15:6) Jesus truly lives!

Write Acts 1:3.

____

____

____

As we finish our journey together, let's examine how the power that God displayed through the resurrection of His Son is the same power that He uses to transform our lives for His glory.

● In what way does our entire Christian walk depend upon the resurrection power of God?

____

____

____

✔ Read I Peter 1:3-9.

In His great mercy, what has He given us? Through what are these precious gifts given?

____

____

Describe the inheritance that is yours.

____

____

● In what way do trials refine our faith? Does this change the way you look at struggles in your life? Explain.

____

____

● Have you ever experienced this refining process? Explain.

____

____

What is the result of this refining process?

____

What is the goal of your faith?

____

● How can staying focused on the shadow of the cross fill us with an inexpressible and glorious joy?

____

____

What wonderful benefits are ours as we come to God through the blood of Jesus Christ! The power of the resurrection provides, through His great mercy, a new birth, a living hope, and an imperishable inheritance. In these three gifts, we find all we need to live lives of praise and service before Him.

The first gift of His mercy that we receive when we come in the name of Jesus is a new birth. This is the transforming work of Jesus' blood.

● Why do we need a new birth?

____

____

How is this new birth accomplished? Acts 2:36-38

____

● In what way is the new birth we receive in Christ the most spectacular showcase for the resurrection power of God?

____

____

Without Christ we are lost. Our sin has made us filthy. We are ruined and without hope. As we come to gaze upon the face of Jesus, we recognize our own unworthiness and helplessness. This is where the love of the cross and the power of the empty tomb extend to us a remarkable invitation. We can shed the old person, corrupted by sin, and become a new person, made acceptable and clean through the blood of Jesus. The resurrection power is spotlighted in the waters of baptism as a fresh, clean, whole person is raised to walk a new life.

The transformation power of the resurrection does not end there. Each day as we depend on His grace, this power is transforming us into the image of Christ. Each day we are once again washed clean in His blood as we seek to shed everything from our hearts that does not imitate Him.

● Where in your life today do you need God's power to mold you into the image of Christ?

____

____

The second gift His mercy gives us is a living hope. This hope is not a wish or far off dream. It is the hope that defines each moment of our lives as Christians.

● What hope do you have in Christ?

____

____

This living hope is a surety about the presence of God in our lives today and the assurance that we will live in His presence tomorrow. This living hope fills our hearts with peace and allows us to view life as a journey, not the destination. Troubles and struggles are put into perspective because our living hope assures us that this world is not our home. It allows us to greet the dawn with joy and the sunset with peace.

The third gift His mercy gives us is an imperishable inheritance. When you became His child, a room in His heavenly mansion was reserved just for you! No one can take that away from you. You can choose to walk away from it, but no robber or thief can steal this joy from your heart.

● How does the surety of your inheritance change the way you deal with the things of the world?

____

____

There is one more gift that provides assurance for our hearts and gives us the strength to face each day.

Read Romans 8:31-39. What great gift does His mercy reveal to us?

____

● How does the death and resurrection of Jesus cement the awesomeness of God's love for you in your heart?

____

____

____

We began this study hearing the melody of Elizabeth Clephane's beautiful song, *Beneath the Cross of Jesus*. As we spend these last few minutes together, close your eyes and let your mind picture all you have learned about Jesus and the shadow of the cross. Holding that picture in your heart, listen quietly to Elizabeth's words.

> *Upon that cross of Jesus, Mine eye at times can see*
> *The very dying form of One Who suffered there for me;*
> *And from my smitten heart, with tears Two wonders I confess:*
> *The wonders of His glorious love, And my own worthlessness.* [3]

Learn to walk each day in the shadow of the cross. Depend on the forgiveness you find there. Rely on the power God demonstrates there. Imprint on your heart the Name of the One who died for you there. Rejoice each day in the redemption that is found there. Commit to living a life that proclaims that the radiance of the Son is most powerfully seen in the shadow of the cross.

---

1 Lockyer, *All the Men of the Bible,* p197
2 Strong, p1114
3 Clephane, p314

Bibliography

Bishop, Jim. *The Day Christ Died*. New York: Galahad Books, 1977.

Carpenter, Eugene E. and Comfort, Philip W. *Holman Treasury of Key Bible Words*. Nashville: Broadman and Holman Publishers, 2000.

Clarke, Adam. *Adam Clarke's Commentary on the Bible*. Kansas City: Beacon Hill Press, 1967.

Clephane, Elizabeth. *Beneath the Cross of Jesus*. 1872. *Songs of Faith and Praise*. West Monroe: Howard Publishing Co., Inc., 1994. Seventeenth printing, 2001.

Coffman, James Burton. *Commentary on Exodus*. Abilene: ACU Press, 1985.

————. *Commentary on Galatians, Ephesians, Philippians, and Colossians*. Abilene: ACU Press, 1977.

————. *Commentary on John*. Abilene: ACU Press, 1974.

————. *Commentary on Luke*. Abilene: ACU Press, 1975.

————. *Commentary on Mark*. Abilene: ACU Press, 1975.

————. *Commentary on Matthew*. Abilene: ACU Press, 1974.

The Daily Bible. Eugene: Harvest House Publishers, 1984.

Davis, John D. *New Illustrated Davis Dictionary of the Bible*. Nashville: Royal Publishers, Inc., 1973.

Edersheim, Alfred. *The Life and Times of Jesus the Messiah, Volume Two*. Grand Rapids: Wm. B. Eerdmans Publishing Co., 1969.

Edwards, William D., M.D.; Gabel, Wesley J., MDiv.; Hosmer, Floyd E., MS, AMI. "On the Physical Death of Jesus Christ". *The Journal of the American Medical Association*. 21 March 1986. Volume 256. www.cga94.com/contributors/stuff/crucifixion/. October 25, 2001.

Halley, Henry H. *Bible Handbook, 22nd edition*. Grand Rapids: Zondervan Publishing House, 1959.

Life Application Bible. Wheaton: Tyndale House Publishers, Inc. and Grand Rapids: Zondervan Publishing House, 1990.

Lockyer, Herbert. *All the Apostles of the Bible.* Grand Rapids: Zondervan Publishing House, 1972.

———. *All the Men of the Bible.* Grand Rapids: Zondervan Publishing House, 1958.

———. *All the Messianic Prophecies of the Bible.* Grand Rapids: Zondervan Publishing House, 1973.

———. *All the Women of the Bible.* Grand Rapids: Zondervan Publishing House.

McDowell, Josh. *Evidence That Demands A Verdict, Volume I.* Nashville: Thomas Nelson Publishers, 1979.

The NIV Study Bible. Grand Rapids: The Zondervan Corporation, 1985.

Strobel, Lee. *The Case For Christ.* Grand Rapids: Zondervan Publishing House, 1998.

Strong, James. *Strong's Exhaustive Concordance of the Bible.* Nashville: Crusade Bible Publishers, Inc., 1894.

Vine, W.E. *Vine's Concise Dictionary of Bible Words.* Nashville: Thomas Nelson Publishers, 1999.

Zodhiates, Spiros, Th.D. *The Hebrew-Greek Key Study Bible.* Chattanooga: AMG Publishers, 1990.

Crucifixion Prophecies

Prophecy	Jesus' Betrayal	Fulfillment
Psalm 41:9	Betrayed by a close friend	John 13:18-26
Zechariah 11:12-13	Thirty pieces of silver	Matthew 26:15
	Money thrown into the temple	Matthew 27:5
	Used to buy a potter's field	Matthew 27:7
Zechariah 13:7	Disciples desert Him	Mark 14:27,50

Prophecy	Jesus' Trials	Fulfillment
Psalm 22:7	Mocked	Matthew 27:31
Psalm 109:2	Accused by false witnesses	Matthew 26:59-60
Isaiah 50:6	Abused, beaten, and spit upon	Matthew 26:67 / Matthew 27:30
Isaiah 53:3 / Psalm 118:22	Rejected by His own people	Matthew 27:22-25
Isaiah 53:7	Remained silent	Matthew 27:14

Prophecy	Jesus' Physical State	Fulfillment
Psalm 22:14	Blood and water flowing from pierced heart	John 19:34
Psalm 22:16	Hands and feet pierced	John 20:25
Psalm 34:20	No bones broken	John 19:33

Prophecy	Jesus' Words From the Cross	Fulfillment
Psalm 22:1	Forsaken by God	Matthew 27:46
Psalm 22:15	Terrible thirst	John 19:28
Psalm 31:5	Commits His spirit to God	Luke 23:46
Isaiah 53:12	"Father, forgive them…"	Luke 23:34

Prophecy	Others' Actions in the Shadow of the Cross	Fulfillment
Psalm 22:7	Hurl insults, shake their heads	Matthew 27:39
Psalm 22:18	Cast lots for clothing	John 19:23-24
Psalm 38:11	Neighbors stay far away	Luke 23:49
Psalm 69:21	Vinegar for thirst	John 19:29
Isaiah 53:9	Assigned a grave with the rich	Matthew 27:57-60

Prophecy	Other Crucifixion Prophecies	Fulfillment
Isaiah 53:12	Numbered with transgressors	Matthew 27:38
Amos 8:9	Sky goes dark	Matthew 27:45

Take Time For Yourself and Retreat Into The Heart of God

Relax, Read, and Reflect as Casandra Martin shows us the way into a deeper relationship with the Father.

Women Opening the Word

ABCs of a Godly Heart - 978-0-89098-300-3
Echoing His Heartbeat: the Life of David - 978-0-89098-301-0
Fragrance of Faith: Discovering the Aroma of Christ in the Beatitudes - 0-89098-297-X
God Pass By Me: Study of the Names of God - 0-89098-257-0
Immeasurably More - 978-0-89098-303-4
Impossible - 978-0-89098-305-8
A Light in the Darkness: Elijah and Elisha - 0-89098-295-3
Living Stones - 978-0-89098-304-1
Our Father in Heaven...Teach Us to Pray - 0-89098-298-8
Paul, By the Grace of God - 0-89098-296-1
Set Free - 978-0-89098-302-7
The Shadow of the Cross - 0-89098-262-7
That You May Believe: the Gospel of John - 0-89098-299-6

Tell Me the Story...

In this series for both men and women, Casandra and co-author Bill Rasco explore your favorite stories of faith from a fresh perspective.

The Armor of God - 978-0-89098-339-9
Meeting Jesus - 0-89098-338-0

The Jesus Resolution
978-0-89098-344-7

&

Living the Jesus Resolution
978-0-89098-343-0

Accept the invitation found in these two collections of devotional thoughts. An amazing transformation occurs when you strive to look like Jesus in each moment of every day. Whether you are doing laundry, washing dishes, or paying bills, you can learn to see God in every place and in every simple task. When God touches the ordinary with His presence, nothing is ever the same. Make the Jesus Resolution and live it today!

(Each Gift Book Contains 120 Devotionals)

$12.99 ea.